ANCESTORS

Divine Remembrances of Lineage, Relations and Sacred Sites

Enjoy these other books in the Common Sentience series:

ANGELS: *Personal Encounters with Divine Beings of Light*

ANIMALS: *Personal Tales of Encounters with Spirit Animals*

ASCENSION: *Divine Stories of Awakening the Whole and Holy Being Within*

GUIDES: *Mystical Connections to Soul Guides and Divine Teachers*

MEDITATION: *Intimate Experiences with the Divine through Contemplative Practices*

NATURE: *Divine Experiences with Trees, Plants, Stones and Landscapes*

SHAMANISM: *Personal Quests of Communion with Nature and Creation*

SOUND: *Profound Experiences with Chanting, Toning, Music and Healing Frequencies*

Learn more at sacredstories.com.

ANCESTORS

Divine Remembrances of Lineage, Relations and Sacred Sites

Featuring

MINDAHI BASTIDA

SACRED STORIES
PUBLISHING

The information provided in this book is designed to provide helpful information on the subjects discussed. This book is not meant to be used, nor should it be used, to diagnose or treat any medical condition. The author and publisher are not responsible for any specific health needs that may require medical supervision and are not liable for any damages or negative consequences from any treatment, action, application, or preparation, to any person reading or following the information in this book.

References are provided for information purposes only and do not constitute endorsement of any individuals, websites, or other sources. In the event you use any of the information in this book for yourself, the author and the publisher assume no responsibility for your actions.

Books may be purchased through booksellers or by contacting Sacred Stories Publishing.

Ancestors: Divine Remembrances of Lineage, Relations and Sacred Sites
Mindahi Bastida
Co-edited by Geraldine Patrick Encina

Print ISBN: 978-1-945026-99-7
EBook ISBN: 978-1-958921-02-9
Library of Congress Control Number: 2022942554

Published by Sacred Stories Publishing, Fort Lauderdale, FL USA

CONTENTS

PART ONE: UNDERSTANDING OUR ANCESTORS

In the Beginning 5

Our Identity 9

The Legacy of Our Ancestors 17

Lineage, Entities, and the Motherlands 25

Sacred Sites and Ceremonies 45

PART TWO: DIVINE REMEMBRANCES OF LINEAGE, RELATIONS AND SACRED SITES

He Who Comes from the Wind *Mindahi Bastida* 59

The Mystical Heath *Cheri Evjen* 63

Experiences of Light in Sacred Sites *Drs. J.J. and Desiree Hurtak* ... 69

Clay and Consciousness *Dr. Kristy M. Vanacore* 75

Teshuvah *Rev. Yael Navid* 81

The Tall Ones *Dr. Kurt Johnson* 85

Staff of Life *Lindsey Uluwehimailani Morriss* 91

Meeting at Serpent Mound *Grandmother Flordemayo* 95

Healing and the Ancestral Bridge *Dr. Julie Krull* 99

The Valley of the Ancestors *Saryon Michael White* 103

Family Contact *Ginny Colarusso* 109

Fly Free *Chris Ciepiela* 113

Ancestral Troops in Wales *Karen Vaughan* 117

Come To Me *Sujon Datta* 125

Avelina *Lucia Goñez* 131

The Christmas Robe *Judy Helm Wright* 135

Life Lessons from Uncle George *Deborah Ann Bustin* 141

Reconnecting to Joy *Florentine Bisschops* 147

The Lite Brite Board *Rev. AnnE O'Neil* 153

The Matchmaking Owl *Nina Mathews* 157

Reflections of Father *Leena Banerjee Brown, Ph.D.* 161

The Healing Light *Mindahi Bastida* 165

PART THREE: DEEPENING YOUR ANCESTRAL CONNECTION

Protocols and Discipline to Deepen Connection 173

In Sacred Connection 187

Final Thoughts and Blessings 199

MEET OUR SACRED STORYTELLERS 205
MEET OUR FEATURED AUTHOR 209

PART ONE

Understanding Our Ancestors

*To forget one's ancestors is to be a brook
without a source, a tree without a root.*

—CHINESE PROVERB

IN THE BEGINNING

At the beginning of time, billions of years ago, all was darkness. Then light emerged, and where all was silence, sound broke through. Galaxies multiplied. Stars and solar systems were created and destroyed. Over 4,000 million years, this planet has become an astoundingly complex and vibrant body. Volcanic activity beneath the oceans formed supercontinents, rifts, tectonic plates, and continental masses. These spread apart and collided, submerged, and re-emerged. In more recent times, all sorts of organic forms have appeared, co-existed, and disappeared.

Some creation stories agree with the scientists that it all began with nothing, a vast, empty space with no sound or light or being. Such is the case of the *Popol Vuh* [The Book of Counsel] that comes from the K'iche-Maya peoples in Guatemala. They believe conscious beings from some other realm arrived to carry out different trials to create a world of creatures that would acknowledge and respect them.

Other creation stories start with a tumultuous world of monsters with massive strength and no sense of purpose. A mother attempts to appease them with the help of her twin sons that she conceives with the Sun. A variation of this second story focuses on one of the monsters and the way in which the twin sons, two Quetzalcoatl serpents, transform the body of the monster, a Caiman, into a world with mountains, caves, water, and a starry sky.

In this story, along with the Caiman's body, there is a turtle that floats in the sea. The Haudenosaunee, the Otomi-Toltec, and the Maya consider this the ultimate motherland and home where the first fire was lit and the first seeds were grown. Among the Mapuche in South America, the twin serpents—Treng Treng Vilu and Caicai Vilu—have antagonistic forces; one works with the mountains, raising them at will, and the other works with the ocean waters. The two maintain a balance that can be broken with the slightest breaching of their mutual covenant.

The Otomi-Toltec carved the enormous basaltic Stone of the Sun (*Piedra del Sol*) to tell of the times lived and predict the times to come; the stone's resistance to the passing of ages shows how important it was for ancestors to mark the closing and opening of cycles. The stone identifies 2012 as the closing of a 5,200-year cycle, the last fifth of a 26,000-year cycle, whereby a new cycle begins on Year One Flint. The flint is the birthing element of Ehecatl Quetzalcoatl himself, so beginning the cycle on Year One Flint in 2012 has meant, for the Otomi-Toltec, that the dawning of a new Sun has begun under the auspices of Quetzalcoatl.

In these times of transition, humanity will be exposed to the unleashed force of the four sacred elements—fire, air, water, earth—while having the opportunity to evaluate their behavior and refresh their covenant with the ancestors. The ancestors have always worked hard to maintain balance and harmony in the world.

HUMAN LIFE ARRIVES

We are the synthesis of all that has ever existed in the universe, our galaxy, our solar system, and in Mother Earth. The huge celestial bodies floating in the cosmic sea are our first ancestors. Equally, mountains, volcanoes, glaciers, and rivers of today are ancient ancestors that are still alive. All the biomass that sank to the sea bottoms and was crushed by the weight of time and rocks has become oil—a special and condensed form of ancestors.

Youngest of all are our ancestors of human origin. These ancestors are said to have come from stars in nearby constellations several million years ago. Oral tradition says that the most recent direct ancestors appeared thirty to twenty-five thousand years ago in Atlantis and Lemuria, two continents now sunken. As Earth's climate conditions became milder, their societies increased in complexity—but when their continents became unstable, they were forced to migrate, taking with them as much knowledge and technological skill as they could.

Native peoples view the process of evolution as beginning with a first mother or a first couple, the "old father and old mother." These individuals always maintained a relationship with the stars. They are considered the parents of everything that exists in the world. In my particular lineage—the Otomi-Toltec—this couple is connected to Makih-Mu. They are thought to have come from the Pleiades, in the region of the sky called Yuh-Mu, to populate the continent Mu. There is even a time marked in the original calendar for the celebration of Mu. The celebration keeps us connected to our first mother and father, Makame and Makata.

Ancestors become important in our lives when we understand that they have handed down to us a significant responsibility: to maintain harmony with nature and the cosmos in every act of our lives. In doing this, we keep alive the teachings about the original principles of life in an evolutionary way that honors our cosmogonic interrelation—our connection to the cosmos.

The teachings give us an opportunity to "know" ourselves and to reconnect with everything that exists that is meaningful to us. The connection helps us understand our identity and how sacred life is. It illustrates the importance of recognizing the root of one's presence in the world. If we know where we come from, we can take responsibility for who we are and we can walk with dignity and care, relating to other beings with wisdom and humbleness.

OUR IDENTITY

Our ancestors build and shape our identity, both in the here-and-now and in the eternal cosmos. Our identity is both tangible and intangible, matter and spirit.

My people say we are made of the flesh of corn, and in other latitudes, our brothers and sisters are deeply connected to and depend on potatoes, wheat, rye, or rice... all sacred plants. Our ancestors co-evolved with these foods, a process that took them thousands of cycles of birth, death, and re-emergence to develop. We are also made of water, which blesses us from the time we are born, and when she falls softly on our crops or lets us glide on her waters. We are made of air, inhaled and exhaled by millions of creatures simultaneously, however unaware we may be of this fact—for perhaps in our life we will only observe our first inhale and last exhale.

The life energy that we feel is the warmth generated by the pulsations of all our cells as they co-vibrate with galaxies, stars, the Milky Way, the Sun, the planets, the Moon, and with Mother Earth. Our Earth generously births, nurtures, embraces, and shelters every single one of her earthlings.

We don't need to understand rationally how all of this has come to be... how a fish, a fungus, a rock, a mountain, a river, a lake, an eagle, or a star were created or what or who they are. When we allow ourselves to live in the mystery, we can fully celebrate life in all her beauty and manifestation. This sounds easy, but it requires a lot of inner work. First, we need to shift this sense of "me" and "myself" to a sense of "we" and "ourselves." Becoming conscious that we are one more in the web of life is key to this inner work. It helps us build our identity, interiorize who we are, and answer within why ancestors matter so much.

In the process of building the collective sense of being in the world, it is good to recall that every human group that has ever come together has had common motivations: guaranteeing sustenance, maintaining shelter, and protecting the continuation of a lineage. This manner of good living is assured when there are wise community members who are in daily dialogue with the spirits of nature. This kind of dialogue prompted the celebration of waters, animals, and plants to become a central aspect of the group's activities, till the practice became tradition. In this setting, every family member, old or young, a midwife or a maiden girl, is assigned a certain responsibility. When that responsibility is met, the community as a whole ensures that there will be plenty, because nature is rejoicing. As everyone learns of their contribution to the common good, they accept rules so that any misbehavior and misalignment with the laws of nature is addressed in good timing.

When everyone participates in such a community, observing their contribution to the common good, it cultivates a deep sense of belonging. This is the most important aspect of identity. When you can proudly say "I am from this community," you are acknowledging all that has made you be the integral being that you are.

Looking deep enough at what makes us who we are, we can see that we are everything that, until now, has left a mark on us. These experiences carry a blueprint, a signature. We are the result of sounds, voices, smells, colors, lights, textures, faces, bodies, and all that stands out in the landscape and seems to talk to us and to those around us. We are all that is in the skyscape, both at day and at night, which seems to feel with us. We are also what comes from our experience with the tangible world and with the intangible world, our dreams and visions. Every experience produces a perception within that makes us reason in a certain way. This reasoning is filtered by a worldview that has come from songs, dances, stories, legends, and myths held and shared by the members of our culture.

Our sense of who we are comes from our participation in activities like fishing, sailing, cultivating, beekeeping, weaving, herding, horse riding, cooking, playing music, dancing, making pilgrimages, partaking in or watching ceremonies, and much more. We love playing our part in these activities because they reinforce the sense of belonging to a group; and we acknowledge the way that the group produces and reproduces interactions with nature, especially when they honor the original principles of living in harmony with everything that is.

Our ancestors felt the same way; they were born in a landscape and prayed and worked and walked the lands and waters in a reciprocal relationship with all the ones living and dwelling there. When they died, they were integrated back to nature or by nature. This integration happened organically. Its meaning was reinforced in songs, dances, and prayers offered by their life companions. Consider here our human companions, as well as birds and animals, who likewise sing, dance, and pray. Even the wind and the waters do this, and even the mountains and volcanoes and the rivers and seas also do. So, for generations, the bodies of our human ancestors have transmuted into the four sacred elements, impregnated with the loving energy of all their relations, and that is why our ancestors considered mountains and creeks, seas, and winds to be their ancestors—and those of us who follow their guidance feel that way, too.

THE MESSAGE OF THE ANCESTORS

Ancestors with strong spirits are capable of appearing in the dream world, and those of us who have the capacity can see, listen, and speak with them. But there are multiple other ways in which they manifest and support us in our life process. They help us evolve so that we can expand our consciousness about who we are and what our tasks and responsibilities are in this world. They show us all of this in what we dream but also in how we feel and taste, and in how we act or perform a song or a dance or any kind of task—especially when it is done with care and love. We can sometimes even see signals in the sky, in the air, in the water, and in minerals. Ancestors are omnipresent, ever present, everywhere present.

Our ancestors tell us how to live in sacred connection. For this, it's important to *feel* beautifully and it's necessary to *think* beautifully, but it's much more significant to *connect* beautifully. Through that kind of connection, you remember who you are, you *know* who you are, and you *celebrate* who you are. You are star dust. You are the balanced combination of the sacred elements. You are at the meeting point of the four directions and a dew drop in a fine thread of the web of life. You are the result of a sacred "touch" from the Divine source.

We hold different stages or layers of identity, both tangible and intangible. Tangibly, we are part of a family, a clan, and a culture. We are also in physical interaction with the place where we were born, the landscape and the territory. The character and vocation that we develop are in relation to the social group that we live with. The ecosystem that we grow in also determines what we feel most attuned to.

Our ancestors have passed down dances, rituals, and popular songs to enrich our identity. For many of us, they are a natural component of our daily lives. Also common in many societies and cultures are festivities celebrated to enjoy specific calendar events. For example, the celebration of the new year means the renewal of the life cycle to many different cultures. Special activities to celebrate both migratory and mating cycles, such as those of whales or geese, sometimes go back centuries. Many rituals happen around the arrival of a new season, such as spending family time with cherry tree blossoms in Spring or with ripe grapes to collect them for wine-making in Summer or Fall. Hence, ceremonial practices are continuous and cyclical expressions that relate the material world to the spiritual.

These practices help maintain the bond of identity over time, and the bond becomes weakened when festivities and celebrations are not practiced. When they are carried out, the sense of community is invigorated among participants. People generally commit to come together again, and so the cycle of life keeps going. At these occasions, most people dress in their local attires and eat traditional dishes. The markets offer a whole display of fruits, meals, clothes, woven materials, art pieces, music, and more. They are the living evidence that what we harvest and how we transform food, fibers, and minerals strongly reflect the region we come from. There is always an imprinting, a seal that marks the provenance of what is made locally in traditional ways.

Our ancestors have also passed down intangible knowledge, such as through languages. Language reflects our relationship with nature, the landscape, and the sky. Language contains the most significant expressions of the collective identity within a bioregion. Languages include the presence of ancestors and the wisdom they offer to the world. When you lose a language, you lose wisdom and identity. You lose the west, the south, the east, and the north. Then you hardly know where you are in the world.

When a language is lost, not only the people lose it, but the whole world loses it. Possibilities of understanding the collective existence are lost, and possibilities of understanding the uniqueness of a culture are lost. For instance, distinctive identity features are part of the written symbols of language. However language is transmitted, it is possible to recognize which region or culture a person comes from by listening to it or seeing it in symbolic form. Even the cosmology of a group is revealed through language, as it creates abstract symbols which allow us to connect with nature and the universe in special ways.

The tales of our ancestors help connect us to manifestations that are between the tangible and intangible, such as mermaids or dragons. These beings are tied closely to the belief of a peoples in relation to mythological figures in creation stories and other narrations. Religious and spiritual practices related to nature are normal among original peoples and are increasingly common among "grounded" communities of faith. In such practices, there is a special relationship with sacred animals, plants, mushrooms, and minerals, and this also makes up one's identity—for you may have more affinity to crystals than to medicinal plants, and so forth.

OUR COLLECTIVE IDENTITY

By giving ourselves space to take a close look at all this, we can rethink the identity we have built as individuals. Identity is formed in relation to family, but also to the community, the town, and the natural environment. Identity is affected by the region, the country, the continent, and beyond. However, it is important to emphasize that the different layers of identity can be built on only if the first layer is well-cultivated and secured. Otherwise, the person keeps feeling out of place. That happens because they have not resonated with any community—and because they have not been guided into taking on a responsibility. Identity forms naturally when you know who you are and where you come from. That is why it is important to know our lineage: where we come from, our original culture, and the collective identity of the culture.

Collective identities among cultures are first formed by landscapes. In ancient cultures, the savannah, the desert, the jungle, the coast, the islands and seas, the forests and volcanoes became our first mothers and fathers. As will be further elaborated, they are our most ancient ancestors, so we honor and pay respect to them; we thank them for being the source all of life, including human life. This acknowledgement gives our identity a *projection*; that is, our original place of reference acquires meaning beyond the self. Then we are better equipped to feel in unity with the diverse planetary community.

In the process of cultivating a sense of identity, we become naturally connected with our ancestors. This experience can heal us if we proceed with care, reverence, and respect, offering permanent co-responsibility with life and a true willingness to transcend. The process shows us how to keep mind, body, and soul in balance, and how to do it in a humble way. When we leave life, we continue to be—as our ancestors are. For we are not here forever in matter; rather, we remain as spirit in continuous transcendence.

Building a strong sense of identity, both individual and collective, is medicine that heals the body, soul, and spirit, transcending time and space. It implies a firm responsibility that directs us, telling us what, how, where, and when to carry out activities. In every activity, we have the opportunity to reaffirm who we are and to evaluate how we are behaving with Mother Earth. Indeed, Earth is our great mother and we owe everything we are to her; likewise, we recognize the Sun, the Moon, and the stars as our elders.

Acknowledging these elements of our identity reminds us that we are not single or alone: we are all our relations.

THE LEGACY OF OUR ANCESTORS

*L*egacy is what is passed on, from generation to generation. It is something of value for the continuation of life. Our legacy gave meaning to the first mother and father of our lineage, in the beginning of times—and when it is presented to us, we are told how to cherish it. To receive and carry forward a legacy is a tremendous responsibility. Its value and significance continue to influence us, because the legacy is who we are. This is one of the ways our ancestors make sure they remain related to us in the present time.

For some people, legacy is encoded in a surname. But for others, the legacy is the love and connection to a mountain, a desert, a wetland, a sea, an ocean, or the sky and any of the animals that dwell in those places. In this kind of legacy, people practice the art of communication with the spiritual beings of those places. The ancestors acknowledged those places to have come first and to be bigger than ourselves.

In the highlands of Mexico some people are given the task of interacting with weather beings (or *meteors*, as climatologists would say), and so they become "hailers" (*graniceros*)—literally, people who can talk with the spirit of hail. They receive special talents or responsibilities to communicate with the sky, to speak with the rain, or to speak with the clouds. When there is going to be heavy rain, they are foretold in a dream; the next day, they burn special herbs and talk with the clouds and the winds. Such is the task of someone who inherits a weather-related legacy. She knows that if she does what she is asked, the rain will come softer or the hail will not destroy the crops because it will fall on the mountains, where no damage can be done.

We can see in this example that when a legacy is passed on, it is not necessarily in the interest of only a family or a town, but rather in the interest of the whole territory. Some people are endowed with wisdom and skills to create balance and harmony with nature. They can take on this responsibility thanks to a spiritual understanding; they know that this is beyond themselves or their free will. These kinds of legacies are especially meaningful, and the holders must honor them. The legacies are not merely a talent, or simply a gift; for those who hold them, there is a deep understanding that the gifts are both talents and responsibilities at the same time.

Another kind of legacy is knowledge about the way of doing certain things, such as playing music or executing certain dances. The art of performing these cultural expressions comes with a big responsibility for those who inherit the skills. People might inherit them through the bloodline, meaning that their grandparents were equally good musicians or dance performers.

But there are also higher responsibilities—let's call them Divine legacies. These don't show up in the family lineage but come from other conscious beings who are in connection with the person chosen to meet the task and be in service. For example, some healers have the task to protect not just people, but whole ecosystems of animals and plants. In such cases, they have a bigger responsibility; special entities guide and accompany them to give their assistance.

Some people are in touch with special spirits. When they close their eyes or go into deep meditation, or when they dream, they receive instructions and special information. They might be given tools and shown how to use them. In this way, our ancestors might pass on a responsibility. This is how we know our ancestors are present, they are conscious, and they influence us in many ways.

UNDERSTANDING YOUR LEGACY

To understand our legacy, we need to connect with the past and the present. We must open ourselves to a mosaic of complex relationships that include special characters and unfinished stories. Each person has an identity; it has been shaped by close and far relatives and members of the community and nurtured by the environment she grew in and related with.

Most people come to know and understand their legacy at family gatherings, where elders speak of their values related to caring for the land; these gatherings provide opportunities to open up for long and rich conversations. Also, some people feel a calling because of certain situations or experiences that happen while they are children, adolescents, or adults. They get affirmations about this calling in dreams or through certain encounters, and then they know that they must take a responsible path to be of service to Mother Nature, to act like a nurturing mother or father themselves.

Sometimes, a person's own mother or father accompany them in this process, reminding the young one about their responsibility in the world and ways to be in service to the community. For example, if an adult in the family is a musician, they will pass some secrets to the young one. Then, when the children listen to music, they will pay close attention, because they have been advised since they were little about what they need to connect with in music.

There are times when we see that our grandparents provided a spiritual service for the light or the Divinity, and now the same task is presented to us as an obligation to fulfill that responsibility. Most of these obligations, established by the Divinity, are manifested through dreams or during a health crisis. These trials can be hard, but they push people to acknowledge mystery and the Great Spirit.

There once was a man who already was married, and this man was getting sick. He received messages in his dreams saying he had to be a healer for the community—not just for his family, but for the whole community.

"No, that's not right, maybe I'm just dreaming," he would say. "I don't know how to do it."

His grandparents had been healers since he was a little one, but he didn't want to pay attention to the calling. He began to suffer when he lost one of his sons. And then many other things happened to his family, and he kept receiving these instructions in the dream time on how to heal people, because he was being forced to take that responsibility.

But he kept saying, "Oh, no, no, but I don't know how to do that. Maybe my grandparents knew, but I don't know."

He had been working in a factory near the community and he began to lose his eyesight. When he was not able to see almost anything, he was taken to some elders in the mountains who were healers. They told him that if he wanted to recover his eyesight, he had to listen to his dreams. He went into a deep training process, and he was healed in such a way that he began to recover his eyesight. He was then taken to a special place by the sea, where there were other people in the same situation, experiencing similar kinds of dreams. They were all there, getting prepared to recover their energy and to strengthen what they had to give.

When he went back to his community, he promised to carry out this mission. He didn't return to work at the factory. He began to perform healing in his house. People from the community began to arrive, and then people from other communities, and from other countries as well. He is still a healer today. For more than thirty years he has carried this tremendous responsibility. He doesn't charge much—just enough for he and his family to live. He is in deep service and rarely leaves the community. It's a huge responsibility, so he cannot travel far.

A few years ago, I invited him to go with us to the sacred sites of Mount Etna, Italy. He said, "I cannot abandon my responsibility because I have people who are coming to see me and they need my support. But I'm going to be with you in spirit."

Indeed, he has a special power: his spirit visits many places around the world, even though he can't travel in body.

These kinds of people exist, and they receive knowledge during dreamtime or while in meditation. Others receive wisdom directly from a thunderbolt or a *centella*, which is a special flash of light sometimes with no sound. In some powerful cases, they faint and receive instructions while they are in a coma, and then continue working the rest of their lives on tasks they are assigned.

These experiences have taught me that when there is a tradition of bondage with the land, people are more naturally prone to providing the community service bequeathed by relatives of previous generations or by the Divine. In this case, there is a harmonious unfolding for the family and the community. But when there is no such bondage or tradition, then the person and the family enter a path of dysfunction, and everything seems to go wrong.

Most families don't understand that they have pending obligations with nature and ancestors. This is particularly true of families that have consistently tried to colonize and dominate in the quest for wealth. For members of such families, reconnecting will require much more dedication and spiritual work.

Some families are accumulating debts to the natural kingdom, either because they never participate in spiritual work related to the regeneration of nature, or because they contribute to destroying the spiritual pillars. They might be morally damaging families who should be responsible for supporting and caring for Mother Earth, or they might be destroying the places where deities receive offerings and payments. These families need to straighten their path. Sometimes, it takes one or two family members to understand the chain of events that has kept them in a state of disgrace and trauma. They need to muster the spiritual strength to guide the family in repairing the damage. Later on we will discuss the practices for this much-needed work.

Those who—in the process of colonization, appropriation, and exploitation of lands, people, and territories—have degraded the atmosphere, the sky, the water, the earth, and the subsoil; those who have caused the banishment of people or partaken in the elimination of populations; those who have imposed religious conversion or promoted the practice of slavery and inhumane industrial labor; all of these people must compensate for the damages caused. This process is absolutely necessary, and it may take generations.

When you and your ancestors have stayed connected with the territory, entities guide you to carry out the actions that are required to maintain the balance and harmony of the place. They also alert you when there is a threat and then instruct you on how to proceed. These entities are natural forces, and they generally have strong characters. In a way, our character and personality reflect the territory's character and personality; that is why we are chosen to work alongside them. In traditional communities, we are familiar with entities and deities; they are present in the collective consciousness, in all sacred sites, and in special places in the waters and lands.

It is a mandate from the ancestors to leave a better world than we received it. Mother Earth is a heritage that is loaned to the present and will have to be passed on to future generations. Biocultural heritage reflects the deep connection and rich relationship with ecosystems, and how it is reproduced and recreated. Biocultural heritage gives identity to the generations that come to be born in a particular landscape. It is an identity that relates to time and space, which is created and recreated by the life of peoples in bioregions and ecosystems in a network between the sky and the Earth.

Though we have a shared identity, we are unique. Identity gives us the opportunity to offer and provide. What we have received from our ancestors, we have to protect and care for, so we can give it to those who come after us. This is how we live between the face of the past and the face of the future. Biocultural heritage is collectively protected, venerated, and respected. The responsibility toward the universe, the Earth, and the place where we were born comes from the origins. It is transmitted from generation to generation. If that responsibility is lost, identity is lost.

That is why we are in the here and now, asking our ancestors to give us strength, wisdom, and guidance so we will not forget where we come from and so we will know what we have to do to transcend and leave a biocultural legacy—because we will be the ancestors of tomorrow.

LINEAGE, ENTITIES, AND THE MOTHERLANDS

ncestors are not just the past; ancestors are the present and the future. That's the mystery we are living in.

The ancestors are the beloved ones. They are reflected in matter but also in spirit, the energetic web of life within the seen and unseen. The ancestors are the lineages that we hold. They guide us and tell us how to solve our difficulties. The love that our grandfathers, our grandmothers, and other family members have for us is most powerfully manifested when we have had the opportunity to talk with them after they have passed away.

Ancestors are the energetic way to connect us with our family lineages, the spirits, and all that is around us. We share an indivisible love connection. The ancestors are the ones who remind us how to live in peace and harmony. They reflect the sacred elements and our connection with the future generations.

When we honor the ancestors, they give us strength and guidance. We must respect our ancestors with honor, responsibility, and reverence.

FAMILY LINEAGE

It is quite common to think about our grandfathers and grandmothers, especially when they have passed away and they were close to us. We remember when they taught us how to behave, how to live, and how to deal with life. And sometimes, we're honored to get to meet our great-grandfathers and great-grandmothers. That is a blessing.

The family lineage goes beyond our grandfathers and grandmothers, from generation to generation. Our community is an extended family that goes beyond the immediate family—yet we are directly connected to them in the same way.

FAMILY AND COMMUNITY

When we talk about our ancestors in the lineage family, we start by thinking of how we connect with our father's side and our mother's side of the family. Some cultures have matriarchal clans and some patriarchal. In original nations and peoples, it's common that they have a complementary way of being. It means that there is a balance. It's not patriarchal and not matriarchal, but it's in between. Our ancestors show us how to live in harmony within the family and in connection with the animals, the plants, and the territory where we were born.

Our ancestors include the ones who are near to us. For example, in a community, it's not just your blood lineage, but also the other families that live near you, because they are also forming you. Our ancestors include all the ones who have passed by who have taught us how to live without conflict, to live with love, harmony, mindfulness, and a consciousness of how to care for life.

Ancestors in the lineage family give us identity, and that identity is a powerful force in the way we live in this world. When we know our identity, we can act in such a way that considers both the seen and unseen forces around us. It's also beautiful to think about the families and communities that are recovering from colonization. Many families have last names that have nothing to do with the responsibility they hold. This is because of colonization; for some people, the names of their conquerors, like the Europeans, were imposed. This needs to be cautiously considered when working in recovering the original legacies of families.

Today, families are recovering their lineages and their remembrance of who they are and who they revere in their prayers and ceremonies. Each family lineage revolves around the connection with some particular animal, plant, mineral, or even celestial body. Some families are related to animals like the bear or the eagle, the tiger, the kangaroo, or the whales. Members of those families respect that connection. That's the reason that families honor their clans. When we hear about the clans of the bear or the clans of the thunderbolt, or those of the whales, the eagles, or the jaguar, we should honor them and show great respect, for it is tremendous work to keep this responsibility going.

Some families are in connection with even more complex beings, such as beings in the sky related to the earth, like the *centella* and the thunderbolt, or beings that dwell in volcanoes like dragons, and beings that live in waters, like mermaids. One in particular has kept me connected with my home: this mermaid is known as the Mother of the Wetlands.

We shall now present different kinds of beings related to the ancestors, like beings of the waters, beings of the caves, and beings of the skies.

BEINGS OF THE WATERS

Some of the enigmatic beings who dwell in water bodies like creeks, rivers, sinkholes, lakes, and the sea are the mermaids. In some traditions, these special beings are considered to be the mothers or fathers of the waters. They are believed to maintain the sacredness of the water bodies and of the plants and animals that live there. For example, the mermaid or *Clanchana*, in my Otomi-Toltec tradition and other like-minded traditions is the one who takes care of all the beings in the water, in the marshes, and in the wetlands, waterfalls, rivers, and the sea.

How do we relate to this being? At least once a year, we carry out a ritual to acknowledge the presence of the mermaid and her vital role in keeping the wetland thriving with life, offering her flowers, fruits, and food. Her existence is not a legend. Some people have had the opportunity to see the *Clanchana* in this tangible, material world because they have the capacity—which is a gift and a responsibility—to see these beings.

My grandfather saw a *Clanchana* twice!

In the year 1932 my grandfather and his son had arrived in his wooden canoe very early in the area called *La Bomba* (the Water Pump). It had that name because the owner kept a part of the wetland permanently dried up with a pump. There, on a morning in late September, as the fog was lifting from the still waters and the ducks and water hens were singing to the rising Sun over the mountain range, my grandfather and his son took off their hats, dipped their hand in the water and bringing it to their forehead, asked permission to the entities and the waters to go in. And suddenly the *Clanchana* appeared.

That day, like others, my grandfather had gone with his eldest son to collect bulrush for his family to weave into mats and other crafts. My grandfather was rowing the wooden canoe through the wetland while ten-year-old Felipe helped with a wooden paddle. Suddenly, they saw a very beautiful woman sitting on a big rock. She was combing her long, shiny hair. From the waist down her body was a long fish tail, and from the waist up she was a beautiful woman. Her skin shimmered in the sun's rays.

Seeing the mermaid is a grace not given to everyone. The two men were stunned. At first they felt scared, but they continued to watch her, not daring to even make a sound. She kept combing her hair—and then, in the blink of an eye, she vanished into the waters.

As they continued to collect bulrush in the following days, they started to wonder if perhaps they had imagined the *Clanchana*. But as they would pass through that place where she had appeared, they would feel a different kind of energy, as if their skin got goosebumps.

About a week and a half after the first occasion, my grandfather was at the ranch of an old colonial settler family. At around 8:00 a.m., the beautiful woman appeared again, seated on a rock in the water. She was combing her hair. When she heard others coming, she flicked her tail and slid back into the water with a great splash.

He never saw her again, but eight days later, he learned that the mermaid had appeared to a neighbor nearby the town of Tlazala.

It's important to be aware and respectful of these beings, for the water is their home. When you don't respect the protocol for going into the lake or to the waters, when you don't ask permission, you can have a bad experience in the water. Failing to carry out the rituals to honor and acknowledge the entities that guard the waters is a negligent act that shows lack of reciprocity. It shows that you lack understanding of this beautiful and complex world of the tangible and the intangible, the natural and the supernatural.

Entities tend to teach us in harsh ways, as do most spiritual teachers. That is why, unfortunately, a disgrace may happen when you don't make an offering of fruits, flowers, and food. It is highly advisable that you prepare yourself and connect deeply before entering waters—because what dwells there is so much more than what is captured by our senses.

BEINGS OF THE CAVES

Some beings dwell in caves. In our cosmovision, caves are cavities through which Mother Earth inhales and exhales. When we are connected, we can see water vapor floating out of caves at certain moments of the day. There, we see that there is an intimate, sacred connection between the wind and the waters. Before you enter a cave, you must ask the permission of the being that dwells there, the keeper of the cave. These beings can take different forms, with both human and animal—or even plant—features.

In many traditions, we need to carry out offerings in caves to recover harmony, so that rains will start on time, and they will be good rains. This ensures good harvests and healthy local economies, and even family issues may be resolved, and community members healed.

In order to carry out these kind of ceremonies, people take on different responsibilities. Spiritual authorities are in charge of presenting offerings or payments, while local people gather flowers, cook special foods, and practice fasting. All this ensures that people have the spiritual strength to interact with entities from the spiritual world and that the families will be in harmony in relation with the ecosystem and the territory.

In some traditions, caves are passages or portals to other dimensions. They are guarded by entities, beings, or deities, and they choose who to let in, depending on the spiritual strength and preparation of the person. Those who are let in are shown abundance of all sorts of cultivated fields, markets, and even taverns full of liquor. People need to be strong in their will to understand what is going on and come out of there as soon as they have taken what is justifiable to take.

Once, in my community, a *mayordomo* (the one in charge of the yearly feast) needed sugar cane stalks for a procession. So he went to the underworld through a cave, and he came out with just enough sugar cane stalks for the procession and the traditional dance and to give away among the community members that attended.

That's why we need to be aware that ancestors are not just legends, and they are not just in stories. Ancestors are fully conscious beings. They are accompanying us, telling us how to live in a good way. They need to ensure we will be good caregivers of the land we have been born into, and even live and die for this territory.

BEINGS OF THE SKY

In the Otomi-Toltec tradition, one of the main heroes is Maxi K'eya, which in the Nahuatl tradition is Quetzalcoatl, the feathered serpent. In other traditions, this being is the dragon deity.

When this ancestor touches someone, they receive a connection from the origins. This person might become a healer or an extraordinary artist. But most of the time, the touch is a calling to become a healer for the community. It's important that we are aware about this kind of touch, because it carries a huge responsibility.

Another set of ancestors, such as the thunderbolt and *centella*, touch us from beyond Father Sky. The thunderbolt makes a loud noise, whereas *centella* is a lightning often without a sound. It can appear anywhere around the world, but it manifests in a volcanic range more often. *Centella* is a celestial power—a power from another dimension that is given to people, animals, trees, and rocks.

One lineage of *graniceros* or (hailers) that I know has been touched by *centella*. This connection is powerful and efficient in giving certain responsibilities to a person. These beings are ancestors as well, and they choose to whom they are going to deliver these powers. A thunderbolt touches with such force that sometimes the person or the animal or the trees are killed. Then they transcend quickly to other dimension, where they can be of even more service to the balancing of the world.

For people to survive a powerful touch like this and live in service, they must become aware of that responsibility and really understand the process of initiation. They need guidance from other people who have been touched by the *centella* or by the thunderbolt, because if they don't carry out this work, mission, or endeavor, they or their families or the community might suffer or become sick.

We need to take seriously what our ancestors are reminding us of: to be responsible and carry out the healing process among families, communities, and among plants and animals. The person who receives the touch from *centella*—or the animal, plant, or minerals that received the touch—becomes strong medicine. This fact helps remind us that we are here not just as human beings. We are nature and other species are related to us.

THE FEATHERED SERPENT

Maxi K'eya (MA-she KE-yah) is the feathered serpent also known as Quetzalcoatl. This entity represents the elements of fire and water. It is also manifested through the rainbow. When we see a rainbow, it's the connection with the heart of Father Sky and the heart of Mother Earth. It represents all the creation that we have in the world.

Quetzalcoatl reminds us of the covenant made with the first mother and father. They are watching from above, from their dwelling place in the Pleiades. Every February 12, we look above us at dusk and see the Pleaides and remember that we are not alone; we are responsible for the continuity of the People of the Corn and the Corn People, for one is made from the other, and vice versa. This communion is practiced in the everyday making of the sacred tortilla, the sacred atole drink, and the sacred tamal. Every February 12, we present the corn cobs to the first mother and father; they are dry and ready for the upcoming cycle of planting, and they are blessed by the first couple, Makame and Makata.

Whenever we have a problem, whenever we have forgotten the instructions brought by Quetzalcoatl, a rainbow appears, thanks to the rainy clouds and the Sun's rays, especially at the onset of the rainy season in early May. The Stone of the Sun shows that the last Sun of the Toltec accountings, which lasted for 5,200 years, ended on December 11, 2012. Now we are preparing to enter a new era in 2026, after thirteen years of cleansing and regeneration.

Five eras have come and passed already. During each one, Quetzalcoatl, the feathered serpent—or his counterpart, Tezcatlipoca, the holder of the smoky mirror—have appeared in person. They have made pilgrimages and given teachings to many peoples in the world, especially in the highlands of Mexico and in the Mayan lands.

It is said that Quetzalcoatl also has appeared in other lands, like the Andes and the Great Lakes. Some even say that he has been in many continents, delivering the messages about our covenant with the first mother and father.

He is an ancestor who has been around for millennia. The prophecy of the new dawn tells us he will be coming back. Over and again, he has been with us, and when we see the rainbow, we remember how to behave and how to bring to the present the original instructions, the original principles.

Quetzalcoatl also goes to other dimensions to deliver messages or prayers as spiritual food for other entities. He is an emissary who tells us how to live in peace and harmony with this planet and with other celestial bodies within the time and space cycles that we live by. That's how we have come to understand that this deity, Quetzalcoatl, is one of the major entities.

TEZCATLIPOCA: THE REFLECTION OF QUETZALCOATL AT NIGHT

Tezcatlipoca is the wind of darkness (*yohualli ehecatl*), a reflection of Quetzalcoatl, who is the wind of twilight (*ehecatl*). Together, they keep forces in the universe in balance. Both keep our connection with mystery. Tezcatlipoca's name means "smoking mirror" in the Nahuatl language. We are to acknowledge Tezcatlipoca as much as we acknowledge Quetzalcoatl. That's how we are instructed to live, conscious of the duality that balances the world.

Tezcatlipoca is a lord of the night. The darkness is a powerful time when most species—including us—go to sleep. But others wake up. Tezcatlipoca is a mysterious entity that puts people to trial and confronts them with unresolved issues. As a smoking mirror, he shows the dark side of things and the world of shadows. By taking on this challenging task, we are given the opportunity to humbly recognize what is valuable in our lives, and to know what we must do to live in balance.

This ancestor allows us to enter a mystery time, especially at night. We know that night is to rest, because it is when life regeneration happens. Now that our body and mind are calm, we can receive messages and become connected with other dimensions. During the dreamtime we might receive instructions or go through a spiritual consultation which is a powerful experience.

Our ancestors communicate during dreams, and Tezcatlipoca is key to access these other dimensions. With guidance from our mentors, we can interpret messages and learn to live during the daytime in a more meaningful, peaceful, and lovely way.

ANCESTRAL DEITIES AND ENTITIES

Deities and entities are our ancient ancestors. Entities are beings; they are spirits that manifest in different ways and take care of a place, in the sky or in the Earth. They manifest to some people when they see an opportunity for mutual acknowledgement. For instance, fairies and other similar beings are entities. They are attentive to our behavior, and they manifest themselves so that we may correct our acts. They are playful and mischievous, like the Aluxes that dwell in the Mayan *monte* or tropical forest and in the *milpa* or cornfield. They throw little pebbles at you to call your attention, and if there is a set agreement about keeping your place in harmony, they will accept sweets, tamales, and a special corn drink.

A deity is a Divine, all-encompassing being, generally associated with an element from the times of Creation. The deities rely on their helpers, which are entities. This is well-known in Mesoamerica, where Tlaloc, the rain deity, has his tlaloques, one on each direction in charge of harmonizing the rains. Their job is not necessarily gentle: tlaloques also cause havoc when they want to change the attitude of a town or a community that is participating in some vice or recurring behavior that erodes local equilibrium.

Deities have dwelled in the same place since time immemorial, even before species of plants and animals existed in this world. They emerged to create the conditions for the generation of life and to harmonize the places where species and natural environments co-evolve. Deities and entities are recognized by the species, in an act of reciprocity. The birds dedicate songs to them, especially at dawn and dusk. Plants thrive in reverence to them. Some human beings offer them spiritual payments and offerings.

When one of the species loses the sacred relationship with the deities and entities, an imbalance occurs. This has happened in general with humans. Many of us forgot about them, either because of a different spiritual practice imposed on us or because of colonization. In such case, the entities manifest themselves to call our attention. At first, they appear in relatively unimpactful events; but over time, if they are not acknowledged, the intensity of their supernatural strength increases to the point of causing serious damage. They can cause illness, accidents, and even the destruction of life.

DEITIES AS CUSTODIANS

In the 1980s, at an entry point to the community called San Pedro Tultepec in central Mexico, strange phenomena began to occur. First there were small accidents, like car crashes, fights between people, bicycle accidents, and other strange things. Then it got worse. At some point, there began to be stronger clashes, and entities started to attack people, depriving them of consciousness. Although they recovered after a while, they were left traumatized.

In a conversation with the community's elder healer, I expressed my concern. His answer was clear: "I know what they are talking about. For a long time, perhaps hundreds of thousands of years, two deities existed in this place. The ancients recognized them through rituals and ceremonies. But about five hundred years ago, a Spanish friar arrived, and he imposed the Christian faith through Catholicism. He had a temple built on top of the holiest site on the island and forbade rituals at the other holy sites, like the cave, the springs, and this place in the town where the deities dwelled.

"The deities endured silence for a long time, until they began to express their disagreement. Then it was learned that accidents were occurring in a second access to the community. Knowing this, we took on the task assuming the responsibility to acknowledge them. Since then, everything has been calm; harmony and balance have returned. There are no more accidents, and everything is at peace," the elder told me.

Something similar was happening on Amsterdam Avenue and between 125th Street and La Salle Street, in New York City. For a few weeks and months, various problems began to arise, to the extent that the patrols were out at night due to fights between people. There were robberies and shootings, among other things. That was when, recollecting what had happened in Mexico, I assumed the task of depositing an offering; at noon one day, I made a deep prayer for the entities that live in that place. I apologized for the lack of recognition, for having forgotten their presence. While I was praying, several people passed by, lost in thought, unaware that I was performing a ceremony. Since that day, the place has been harmonized and free of accidents. But who will take responsibility in the years to come?

This is what happens in many parts of the world: an imbalance occurs, caused by negligence and a lack of knowledge and understanding about the ancestors of the territory and the sacred sites. Then chaos ensues. That's why it is very important to carry out ceremony to acknowledge the deities and entities.

FIRE DEITIES AND ENTITIES

On every continent, there are fire beings that dwell in volcanoes. Their nature is fiery and in many cultures they are seen as dragons. In the highlands of Mexico, they call them Maxi K'eya or Quetzalcoatl—the snake with feathers and wings that dwells in places with fire and water. They are beings that are taking care of volcanoes, and they are our ancestors as well, because they were here before us, before we were present in this world. The fire beings also bring the rain. They bring the warmth of the Earth and they also bring much balance in this world. They produce the energy so the animals and plants can thrive, and even minerals are activated.

When there is a disruption in the ecosystem or a serious problem, these beings are energetically present to compensate for the imbalance. They also call other entities associated with the sacred elements to purify the world by causing earthquakes, tsunamis, and hurricanes, among other events.

Some sacred sites in the world have been revived and protected. Spiritual leaders of the Kogi and Otomi-Toltecs went to Mount Fuji in Japan in 2017, to help heal damage from the nuclear reactor accident in 2011. While carrying out the ritual ceremonies, during which offerings and payments were given, one of the Kogi leaders shared with the group a vision he had been receiving. Two dragons came out of the Fuji volcano to contain the danger and protect land and sea from radiation; they had been exhausted for several years. The ceremony gave them spiritual food and recognition of their work, and they recovered their strength.

Beings of fire are also in close relationship with other beings linked to the sacred elements of life, such as water, air, and earth. The elements work together. In different territories and cultures of the world, they have their own names and characteristics. In general, they are winged beings, but their physiognomy, size, and appearance vary widely.

For all entities, the main deity is the sacred fire. In some peoples of the world, he is represented as an old man or grandfather, known as a fire grandfather. He is wise and gives advice on how to face the complex problems of life. The fire father gives serenity and confidence, and above all enlightens the conscience and brings families and communities together to exchange words. It also helps purify in disease treatments. But when there is tension in a territory because nature was improperly managed, this deity manifests itself in different ways to maintain balance. One of the strongest is when fire devastates forests and populations. Over time, balance is restored and life regenerates.

MOTHERLANDS

We are the reflection of the territory where we are born. What we call land is not just the land where we live, it's the heart of the Earth; there is a heart in every mountain and river, in every desert and oasis, and that heart spreads beauty and love. That's why we feel so connected. The ancestors are always around. They are entities and spirits that dwell in volcanoes, in mountains, in wetlands, in rivers, in the sea, and in sacred valleys. They are authorities that we address with reverence. We dedicate time listening to them so we can heal and recover strength to carry on. These personalities guide us and bring us consciousness about how we are co-evolving with Mother Earth and the universe, and understanding that identity is dynamic, not static.

How many people eventually ask, "Why was I born here, with this family? Why was I born here in this desert or in this forest or in this city or this mountain?" But then they don't go deep for answers. These questions are important because the answers point to our ancestors and to our responsibilities.

There is a deep reason why we are born into a specific place, in a certain community and a particular territory. There is also a reason why we are born into our families. It has to do with the opportunity to establish a direct connection with the ancestors.

A shared responsibility is meant to run unbroken in the lineage. Our ancestors were responsible in the beginning of time, and ideally, there is a legacy that has been honored and carried till today. In this ideal condition, mandates or principles of origin are fulfilled, and the collective personality that gives us a place in the world is thus reinforced.

Some people have lost, or are losing, that connection. They do not know what lineage they come from nor recognize their relationship with the territory and its ecosystems, landscape, and sky. They don't know about their relationship with the bodies of water and the Earth.

One must recognize oneself not only by the lineage one is born from, but also in relation to the landscape, the mountains, the bodies of water, and the points where the sun and moon rise and set. By recognizing ourselves in the dance of these ancestors, we can reconnect with those who practiced multiple forms of bonding. We have the opportunity to find that root. If the person, community, or family needs to relocate—either due to *force majeure* or voluntarily—once relocated in the new place, they must recognize those who were there before. They must find out how to name the town and more importantly, how to name the ever-present authorities of the landscape—the mountains, prairies, desert, jungle, or sea. Also, they can learn how to honor them as part of their activities around the seasons of this new place.

Everyone has the opportunity to recognize themselves through their ancestors by investigating their biocultural history. They can consider their lineages, clans, or sense of belonging to a peoples in relation to the ecosystem, the seas, and the stars. What happens when we know that a relative deeply broke the bond with the ancestors or the relationship between nature and Mother Earth? How does that act—and subsequent events—affect our collective life history as a family? How will it affect our descendants? What can we do to repair the damage we cause or that is caused by our predecessors, and even by our relatives today? Fortunately, ways do exist to heal our ancestral lineage.

SPIRITUAL AUTHORITIES IN MOTHERLANDS

The mountains are spiritual authorities that guide us if we are in deep connection with them; so are the wetlands and the springs, the seashores, and the lagoons. They tell us that we were born there for a purpose, and they give us our identity. We are people of the mountain, people of the islands, people of the desert… when we say "people," we refer not just to human beings, but also animals, minerals, and plants.

The reason we are born in a location, in a specific time and space, is related to responsibility. It is also related to connection: a connection with the sacred elements of life and with sacred spaces and sacred sites.

We believe and we understand that the main reason we are born in a certain place that has a certain energy and character, is because we have something to offer. We must work to provide protection to the place, just as it protects us all. We need to live in reverence, respect, and responsibility with that place or sacred site. We need to give care and take care, because in that way, we will get to know and develop great sensibility for our place, and that's how our identity is built.

Also, when we know the language of the place, we learn so much more about where we live. For instance, we learn that the different names of the rain are according to the direction it comes from and the winds that bring it.

Soon, it becomes more natural to be in connection with those natural phenomena, so when there is some kind of tornado or a very destructive, heavy rain, we know how to ask in a sacred way for balance to prevail; by doing that the rains will not destroy the crops or the shelters of animals or other houses. And when there is lack of rain, or the dry season is too long and there is no rain, we carry out other rituals for the rain deities and entities to act.

That's the connection we have. The connection is established through awareness and a conscious way of being. And that connection is sometimes reinforced in our given name, especially when it holds the identity and legacy of our birthplace. When you have accomplished something where you were born and you have the opportunity to go elsewhere, you need to develop a connection with that land or territory. Responsibilities follow you, so the sacred connection grows in you. If you left your motherland and you don't cultivate that connection, then you are not going to be able to live in a sacred way. Your life may be miserable and empty of meaning.

The motherland gives you the deep connection, the spiritual and material connection. All of us can be proud of the collective identity developed through that connection. That's how we are to live in this world. It is good to be reminded that we can learn from each other with this principle in mind. When you have a strong identity, you have something to offer to animals, plants, your culture and even other cultures and other people. That is reciprocity at work.

The motherland gives you that flavor and color that you can then share with others and feel joyful about. That's why we say, if there is a color lacking in this world, there is no rainbow, and if there is no rainbow, there is no transcendence. Humanity needs a wide diversity of flavors and colors, and in order to share your own, you need to be fully present in their celebration. Mountains, the river, the sea, or the desert, all imprint a powerful way of being, and thanks to that, you can know who you are. Your identity is molded starting with the place you were born and the way you were born and raised. It becomes richer as you evolve with your surroundings.

That's why motherlands and our connection with sacred sites in the motherlands is so significant. There's pure energy in our connection with the universe, and that connection is produced easily when the heritage is alive in you. You enjoy the connection more when you are aware, when you know who you are and where you come from.

How do we know that we have a special connection with a motherland? Sometimes, when you visit a place and it feels familiar, it may be because of a connection coming from the origins or because it is related to the lineage you come from. The place is in the collective consciousness of your lineage—which in turn, gives you a particular way of feeling and thinking. Your human ancestors are telling you that in past times, they were there, too. Through the connection you begin to remember that you have been there before, and you cherish the place. You know that by being in that place, you are experiencing a connection from the past.

When you go somewhere and immediately feel love for the place, it is because the place is giving love. The place acknowledges you, and a bridge of connection or reconnection is created. Sometimes, when you go to places where you feel connected with the heart, there is no explanation. You have no rational way of explaining why you feel that love or that special energy.

Also, when we see butterflies in some special configuration, our ancestors are telling us that they were here, and they are still here. If you visit a cave or a special mountain, and you see the Sun through a certain crack on a specific date and time, then you get a connection—because it's telling you that ancestors also observed this phenomenon and used it as a marker for the corn cycle or the rain cycle. Everywhere around Mother Earth, those signals and messages are being replicated.

When you feel that love, when you feel that deep connection, it is because your lineage, your main lineage, has been in touch with those places, those waters, or those valleys…and you are just remembering that you have that connection, not just from this lifetime, but from other lives. That's a deep teaching of our ancestors. They remind us that we are not alone.

Motherlands are giving us the opportunity to cultivate a special connection to the specific place and time that we were born in. We also are related to sacred places and shrines, wherever we are born. Let us talk about sacred sites now.

SACRED SITES AND CEREMONIES

*S*acred sites are places with special energy vibration. They have important beings and entities as caretakers. Sacred sites are important because natural and spiritual phenomena take place there, and because these sites are collectively acknowledged. People make pilgrimages to such places as acts of energetic reciprocity. This means that sacred sites provide special energy to people, but also people return this special energy, so there's an energetic reciprocity.

Sacred sites have tangible and intangible attributes, and they are associated with time and space. Many sacred sites align with the rising or setting Sun, the Moon, and Venus. These sites are interrelated to specific times and spaces; the ancient observers chose the sites precisely, so that ceremonies would have good outcomes, like rains or good harvests.

Sacred sites orient people about how to live in peace and harmony. Sacred sites anchor time and space at a vortex, and when you are there, you can experience a sense of oneness and expansion of consciousness. You may seek that state by praying every day and asking for guidance at night, but these sacred sites are like a key or a door. They provide a channel to connect with those entities and energies in a more significant way.

People on pilgrimages to sacred sites deliver offerings, carry out rituals, and experience healing. Sacred sites are also the places to ask for good rain, for good weather, and for the protection of crops.

One important consideration for sacred sites is that local people promote community conservation. Since everything is sacred around these powerful sites, people must respect even the little rocks and the little plants, fungi, or animals living there. We cannot remove even a pebble because everything there is sacred.

Visitors must always ask permission to enter any place, even if they have been there before. If it is a sacred site, they need to give offerings. And if you are going to take something from a sacred site, you must ask for permission and listen carefully for the answer, which may be 'no', or may be 'yes', but with a condition to perform a task that will benefit the sacred site enormously. There will be special places where you can return whatever you have taken, and this will represent a special offering or payment for your pilgrimage.

The original nations and peoples greatly appreciate the sacred sites. They should be acknowledged by everybody, because they are related to our origins and offer special energy. Sacred sites help life regenerate so that plants and animals can flourish. They can help us, the human species, to flourish. When we are at sacred sites, we have a saying: "Our ancestors are watching us."

BIOCULTURAL SACRED SITES

Most sacred sites are formed naturally and are related to sacred elements of life. Some sites are more related to the water, in which case other elements—like soil, wind, or fire—also are present, but may be so in less quantity.

Natural sacred sites are venerated because they are associated with both ancestral territories and people. They are honored because they relate to creation myths and to primordial Divinities. Most of these sites have guardians, called caretakers or caregivers, and it's important to understand their role.

Most natural sacred sites include ecosystemic elements or natural structures, such as caves, rocks, a mountain, a river, or a waterfall. The animals and plants dwelling there are also very special.

Many sacred sites are related to deities such as the deity of the rain, or the deity of the wind, or the deity of the mother of the waters. In some cases, monuments are built at these sites and they are placed under the category of cultural sites. But our understanding is that these kinds of sacred sites are both natural and cultural. Moreover, natural sacred sites are *biocultural*, because even if the site is a cave or a waterfall, it has been given a name and holds cultural meaning.

Both natural and cultural sacred sites can in fact be considered *biocultural* sacred sites because of how they are intertwined in our cosmogony. For example, a natural sacred site—such as the Kilimanjaro volcano, the Fuji volcano, or Mount Shasta—can be very significant culturally as shown in its name and in the kind of pilgrimages that are carried out. And the same happens in cultural sacred sites, for even if there is a construction or a monument in the middle of the mountain, the mountain is still the one making the place special. For example, many monuments or constructions such as ceremonial centers, have a spring underneath or a river circling the sacred site. So to us, every sacred site is biocultural because it implies both nature and culture.

We have many examples of biocultural sacred sites, including the volcanoes that I mentioned—Mount Fuji, Mount Etna, Mount Kilimanjaro, Mount Shasta, Mauna Kea, and so on. Some mountains are also biocultural sites, sacred sites. In Asia, we have Mount Everest; in the Andes, we have Ojos de Salado; in South Dakota in the US, the Black Hills; and in Mexico, El Cerro de La Campana. And there are sacred islands like Isla del Tiburón in Mexico, Okinoshima Island in Japan, and the Niuatoputapu in Tonga.

Sacred deserts include the Sonora desert in Mexico or the Atacama in Bolivia and northern Chile; there is the Sahara in Africa; and the Gobi north of China and south of Mongolia. Most rivers are sacred too. All around the world they are sacred at their source, like the Ganga in India, the Fraser in Canada, the Bio Bio in Chile, and the Yangtze in China. Sacred lakes include the Yamdrok in Tibet and the Patzcuaro Lake in Mexico.

Caves are also sacred sites, such as the Ellora caves in India, the cave in Dambulla, Sri Lanka, and the caves in Chalma, Mexico. And also, we can find sacred springs, such as those in the valley of Tolantongo in Mexico. There are also so many sacred valleys throughout the world.

We can find biocultural sacred sites around the world that have been significant for thousands of years, like the pyramids in Egypt, in Tikal, Guatemala and Teotihuacan, Mexico. These are also ceremonial centers, but they are built around a sacred river or mountain. Some important biocultural sacred sites are sanctuaries, like the Taktsang in Bhutan, Esquipulas in Guatemala, and La Villa de Guadalupe in Mexico. Even some communities are considered sacred, like Peña de Bernal in Querétaro, or Lol Tun in Puuc Region in Yucatán, Mexico.

Sadly, these important sacred sites are at risk because some are abundant not just because of the energy flowing from the minerals, the rocks, and the crystals, but also because of precious metals and precious waters that are monetized. Corporations and even some communities want to carry out fracking, mining, or logging in these sacred sites to remove the precious stones or other valuable materials.

GUARDIANS

Sacred places have two different kinds of guardians. The first are ancestral guardians or helpers of ancestral guardians, which means ancestors. These are represented by beings or entities that dwell around the sacred place and show up in various forms. It can be a being or an entity that has its own name–and there are many names for them, depending on the culture and place. These guardians are entities and deities that are there for a specific purpose: to protect sacred sites. These protectors embody the energetic presence of our ancestors.

The second kind of guardians are men or women appointed as guardians by the community or by the ancestors. They are strong people who have been given the responsibility to take care of a place and carry out ceremonies. They may receive instructions about how they must perform a special ritual or ceremony during the year according to the calendar, or according to visions they have seen during the dream time.

HONORING THROUGH CEREMONY

It is important to remember that sacred sites are related to the presence of entities and deities, which are our ancestors. They are dwelling there, and we have the responsibility to visit and honor them. There are special dates for when we must visit or carry out a pilgrimage because that is when time and space intersect. In those moments, the presence of our ancestors is more vivid and present. That's why there are special ceremonies carried out on specific dates when the Sun or Moon or Venus show in certain ways, illuminating specific points. That is when these sacred sites become powerful and full of energy. Both the sites and the people around them are strengthened at this time. Time and space are important in this correlation of forces.

Caves are special because they connect us with the underworld or with ancestors of the very ancient past. The tops of the mountains help connect us to the dimensions that are superior. At certain astronomical times, powerful energies emanate from intermediate points between caves and tops of mountains to produce harmonization and 'recharging' for those interacting with them. These are called the *neuralgic points*. A high level of energy is born in those sacred sites that are the neuralgic points of Mother Earth. These points maintain balance, harmony, and cohesion—in particular, biocultural cohesion. They also provide the opportunity for intercultural exchange, because many of these sacred sites hold not just one culture, but many cultures. The animals and plants at sacred sites can carry messages to us. I have seen, for example, the presence of butterflies in sacred sites, which tells me of the manifestation of ancestors.

When we venerate caves, we know that they open to other dimensions around May 3. This is also when our ancestors are present. And the same happens when we carry out festivities for the Day of the Dead around November 2, which is half of a year later. When we are in connection with those who visit from underworld, just for a little while, we are acknowledging that we are not alone, that we come from those origins. The touch with those ancestors is gentle and delicate; when we deliver special sacred food–spiritual food–they are fed and feel acknowledged. We do this knowing that otherwise they may produce some disorder or discordance in our world. The same happens when we go to the top of the mountains and speak with the superior entities, asking that harmony and balance be secured.

Sacred sites, the underworld and other dimensions, are important. They are essential for humans to have a good living, as they help maintain social and spiritual cohesion. They sustain life and give us conditions for a good living through the reproduction of life itself. That's why, when we go to a sacred site, we feel that we are not alone; in these sites, the presence of our ancestors is powerful, and we feel that we can receive guidance, strength, and energy to continue our lives.

CERRO DE LA CAMPANA

In the Otomi-Toltec territory in the highlands of central Mexico, there's a place called *Cerro de la Campana*—the Bell Mountain. This sacred mountain has special rocks and formations that are like rock balls filled with water. My family walks to this place in sacred pilgrimage. My personal experience is that, on our way to the top of the mountain, we visit many rocks. We bring fruit, bread, and flowers as a way to acknowledge those sacred rocks.

During the whole journey you can feel a powerful energy, but at the same time, it is difficult to walk. You feel joy, and you have enough love to carry this out—but you have to concentrate to think only beautiful, beautiful thoughts. This state of meditation is a practice that can stop negative thoughts from taking over. As you walk, you are chanting and dancing with others at every sacred rock.

When you arrive finally to the top of the mountain, you will find special rocks that were placed there in ancestral times for a reason. They all have little holes; most of the ones I have seen and counted have seven holes, representing the seven sisters of the Pleiades.

Upon arrival, we pray and place offerings of sacred, spiritual food. You can feel how your energy is renewed; even if your body is very tired, you can feel that energy in your spirit. That's how you can really feel that ancestors are present and that they manifest in these places. This experience happens on special dates, based on some alignment between the sun, the moon, and these sacred sites.

I have felt that powerful and deep connection with the mountain as a being when I am on the top of this mountain or at special rocks along the way. I can feel how they transmit an energy and I get a sense of connection. You can even feel the warmth, an energy that fills your whole body and mind.

On our way to Cerro de la Campana, there is a particularly important spring where healing occurs. Sick people can be healed there through prayers and also with the spring water. This water feels cold because it's alive and comes from the mountain; even though it's cold, you can feel the medicine in your body.

Sacred sites *are* our ancestors, and they are taking care of us; in reciprocity, we must take care of them. And that's a beautiful thought to bear in mind: there is a great deal of work that we must carry out as a responsibility to sacred sites.

Our ancestors are alive. They have consciousness and they can distinguish between a work that is coherent and one that is not. They can connect well with those who carry out coherent work in their microcosms, the people who know that their work will co-vibrate with the macrocosms and help intensify and expand the sound of the universe.

Being fully conscious about the repercussions of our acts in the world of the ancestors is crucial. Today it has become imperative that we review our acts and enter into dialogue with those who are family to us. The richness of our identity is in the scope of our relations to elements of time, space, life, and death. We are alone when we cannot name those around us, even if the house or the community is full. So let us give ourselves time to acknowledge all those who have enabled us to become who we are and who can further enrich us to a point of joy.

Let us bring ancestors to the present by weaving in their heroic acts as we invite our family or our community members to share stories. When we become more aware of how vital they are in our lives, we will feel that, whenever we need something, ancestors will act in a way that their presence is vividly felt. That's how we know they are always among us and are eternal. Their manifestation affirms that we are in a web of consciousness and energy that maintains alive the pulse of the universe, the warmth of the Sun, and the heartbeat of Mother Earth.

Listen now to some of the mystical experiences lived by those who have chosen to share their stories with us.

PART TWO

Divine Remembrances of Lineage, Relations and Sacred Sites

And when I breathed, my breath was lightning.

—BLACK ELK

HE WHO COMES FROM THE WIND

When I was only three months old, a miracle saved my life.

I had been born into a large family of musicians. My parents and siblings and I lived in a little bulrushes (tule) house on the property of my grandparents. I slept in a little bed with my mother.

One night, while my father and oldest brother were away with the family band playing music, my mother awoke at about three in the morning to realize I was gone. She could no longer feel my warm little body next to her. She tried to get up to look for me, but a heavy energy wouldn't let her open her eyes.

She was so desperate, that she began praying: "Please help me, because I don't feel my baby. Please help me to get up."

Then she was able to open her eyes, but it was still quite dark. She woke up the other children, who slept on mats on the floor, and they all searched for me in the darkness. My mother stretched her hands over the mattress, under the blankets, desperately trying to feel me. She found me under the bed. I had rolled all the way into the corner, on the freezing cold floor.

My little body was already cold. I was not breathing—I was already dead. She pulled me out and started screaming and crying so loudly that our neighbor, Don Cruz, came running.

"What happened? What happened?" he asked.

"My son cannot breathe! Maybe the witch came, the witch who wanted to take him," she said.

Don Cruz held me upside down by my tiny ankles and began to shake me. I wouldn't react. My mother was screaming in agony. The other children were all crying. It was hard for them. Don Cruz kept trying to revive me, but I was gone.

And then something special started to manifest in the air. As my mother tells me, a huge, swirling wind formed around our little bulrushes hut. It moved the trees and shook all the houses; it was so strong. This wind came right to us.

My mother stood outside, holding me in her arms, praying that I would catch my breath again as the wind blew against us so hard that she could barely stand. Suddenly, this wind went into my lungs, through my mouth and through my nose. It went into my body—and it woke me up. The spirit of the wind came to give me my life back.

That is why my name is Mindahi, which means "he who comes from the wind." My name honors that special moment. The wind became my sacred element that gave me strength. Always, always I can feel the wind in my life. Its energy came to my body, a special energy, and even now it gives me so much power. I have been in connection with it from that day.

So, I was able to come back, I became extremely aware of many things in life. The wind had given me that notion of consciousness.

My first remembrance is from when I was not even one year old. My mother was carrying me on her back, walking on her way to grind the corn to make tortillas; she took a bad step and fell down. I remember seeing the soil coming toward my face as we fell. It was so impressive that I remember that episode, and I was not even walking yet.

By the time I was four years and a half, I could understand most of what my mother was saying. I could already read and write when I started elementary school.

The wind is in my origins. The same wind that creates the movement in the universe is also inside of us. My experience of this has been so strong because that's my ancestry. I give reverence to the wind as a sacred element, but also as a father. Our ancestors are the fathers and the grandmothers, but not only in human form. They could be the sacred elements, as in my case, or it could be a mountain or other sacred beings.

I began my life again after a sacred touch. It was a spiritual way to encounter a mystery in the physical world. It was magical as well because we cannot understand how all these things happen. We have no explanation for this sacred phenomenon that saved me when I was a little one.

Mindahi Bastida

THE MYSTICAL HEATH

*S*tanding on a deep sandy path in Northern Germany's famous Lueneberg Heath Nature Park, I felt an indescribable connection to the local landscape, which seemed a wonder to me as an exchange student from America. Rolling, sandy hills were interspersed with clumps of tall green grasses and plentiful heather plants, their deep purple stems cloaking the hills in vibrant color.

After several hours of walking, the Heath all around me boasted endless views of the sun-kissed heather sprigs, their stems glowing as if encrusted with precious stones from the sunlight dancing off them. It would soon be my turn to dance, but on the inside, as the heath gifted me on an August day with its energy and a view into ancestral worlds that a 16-year-old rarely glimpses.

The heather blossom's intoxicating sweet scent hung in the air. The stunning views were interrupted only by an errant pine or silvery birch tree, with a strip of deep green brush and trees on the far horizon. Suddenly, I became rooted to the heathland as a pulsing energy began to be emitted from the sandy path. The sensation reached up through my feet, into my legs, torso, and heart. I stood there as if alone, the fellow hikers in this vast area fading from awareness while I connected deeply to the land, and its timeless whispers.

The lure of Germany first captured me as an 11-year-old who found the language easy to learn. Fascinated with German culture, heritage, and history, I was fortunate to spend a high school summer in Northern Germany as an American Field Service exchange student, where I soon felt like I was home.

Up until the nature park visit, life on a small dairy farm had seemed simple, yet fulfilling. I enjoyed helping my host family make daily excursions to milk their small herd of white and black Holstein cows by hand as they grazed in nearby pastures. I appreciated the century-old farm with its combination house and barn under one enormous, straw-thatched roof. And the land that was so flat that one could see to the horizon over the small, lush pastures of nearby families, see to where the deep green grass met the clear, robin-egg blue sky.

My host sister and instant good friend was just a year older than I on this warm August day. The wide tires of our heavy, old bicycles hummed with purpose as early in the morning we peddled down narrow country roads that carried few automobiles, cherishing our freedom from farm work and adult supervision. We sped to catch a train from the nearby village, sneezing and laughing while inhaling the fragrance of freshly cut hay and shouting "Moo!" at grazing cows in lush, green pastures. It was exciting to venture to the Lueneberg Heath, the largest of its kind in Central Europe, stretching from Oldenburg to Bremen to Hannover.

Once aboard a train to a neighboring town near the famed Heath, we settled into its gentle swaying rhythm as we spied cotton-ball clouds out the windows that drifted slowly above us in a bright blue sky, their shapes slowly casting playful shadows upon everything below.

Because no cars were allowed in the heathland area, we linked arms upon arrival and strode off, our feet sinking into the warming sands of the path leading to the amethyst-bejeweled hills ahead. A pair of stocky ponies whose coats matched the path color surprised us with their camouflage as they crested the first hill we reached. Their broad heads hung low, eyes hidden by their long forelocks that floated up and down with each step. Attached to the ponies was a small wooden wagon bearing tourists, and we stepped aside to let the ponies with their gentle four-beat cadence and wobbly wagon load pass by.

The intense August sun bore down on us for the first hours of walking into the beauty of the rolling, tufted, blooming landscape. Small herds of shaggy Heidschnucken sheep appeared around a bend, roaming at will across the heathland while grazing upon wayward weeds and tree shoots. The sheep barely raised their heads as we strode by, our shoes coated with glittering golden sand like pixie dust.

One could feel Mother Nature's presence here, singing to her fields of heather and laughing at the shaggy sheep munching the day away. The mystery, the life power of the Heath, caused me to suddenly stop as I felt a shift, a type of mental swoon. The pulsing energy from the path rose in my body as the people on neighboring paths disappeared from my vision. The Heath itself shape-shifted, transporting me to another time.

I was on these same hills, but without the walking paths. Larger birch and pine trees had sprung up before me, clustered haphazardly around the borders of the heath fields and within them. I looked down, bewildered that my feet now sported coarsely carved wooden clogs with blunt tips that peeked out from underneath a long, dark, plain skirt.

My dazed mind picked up a lovely, soft whisper of *Remember!*

Remember what? I silently replied. But to whom?

Remember! The whisper commanded me. *Remember!*

Visions swept over me, as I stood still, trembling. I had walked this heath many times before in various lifetimes. I was the young peasant girl in the dark skirt and wooden shoes, gathering firewood and picking sprigs of heather to sell at a market to help feed my family. I saw myself searching among the trees for small fallen branches, which snapped loudly as I broke them for bundling to carry home. My hands were dirty and calloused, and my nails were torn in jagged edges. The bundle of sticks weighed upon my shoulders and back, and broken branch tips dug into my skin through the loose blouse. The fragrance of the pines and heather blossoms filled my nostrils.

Then the Heath appeared to rise in a waving roll, changing the landscape and showing a vision of myself as a teenaged boy in tattered pants that reached only to my calves. Looking down as the boy, I saw wrinkled, old hand-me-down leather boots that were much too large for me. The cold iron of a long gun was in my arms, with my grip tight on the wooden stock as I tripped over the primitive trails from the oversized boots making it slow going. From hunger in my belly, I knew that I was hunting for rabbits on the rolling hills.

The Heath shifted yet again, and the air moved around me. Gazing about, I made out the shapes of uniformed German soldiers brushing past me into the deepening twilight as they crushed the fragile landscape, marching onward to another conflict. One soldier stopped right before me, his back to me. His long, woolen coat of gray was draped over the grasses and heather. He turned and his gaze startled me, seeming to look right at or through me. Suddenly, I felt myself moving forward with him as he turned and marched to catch up with the others. I was now a soldier in this patrol, full of fear, hunger, thirst, and exhaustion as my booted feet bore me forward. The only sounds came from the grasses being flattened by our boots, and an occasional clink of a metal canteen hitting against belts and guns.

Remember! the whispering voice insisted.

"Cheri?" I heard my name being spoken louder, and close to my ears.

The sound brought me back from my sleep-like journey to a foggy awareness of my own body, and of a woman talking to me. I turned to my host sister. Apparently, she had asked a question that I missed.

"Ja?" I finally croaked, still wanting to keep the mystical feelings and visions with me.

Yet I had been pulled out of the Heath's embrace. The Heath had let me go after fulfilling her goal to help me remember.

Once again, I noticed older women in sturdy skirts with walking staffs on the nearby paths as my vision refocused on my 16-year-old self's surroundings. I was back in virtually the same place and time based on their positions on the path. What had seemed like an hour of visions to me must have lasted just a few seconds.

Despite being dazed, I managed to return more fully to the present time as we retraced a pathway back to our starting point and I began processing my visit to the mystical Heath. I spoke nothing of my experience to my host sister, deciding to keep this special memory private. It was a gift to me from the Heath, and I cherished it.

The Heath had reminded me of previous lives and, to return that honor, I struck upon the perfect idea before drifting off to sleep that night. In repayment to the Heath for opening my eyes to mysticism, I promised that, if I ever had a daughter, her name would be Heather. And so, I now have a living memorial to the Heath, as well as everlasting gratitude for the landscape that helped me remember my eternal self.

Cheri Evjen

EXPERIENCES OF LIGHT IN SACRED SITES

Indigenous elders have always known about unique energy portals and established their temples at certain sacred sites where they experienced unusual light phenomena. We have noticed as researchers visiting such sacred sites for over 30 years that pyramid structures are often positioned at key sites globally that have been popularly called grid or vortex points. These locations serve as unique energy portals to achieve the opening of interdimensional doorways.

These places are sacred because an energy portal opens to other dimensions, allowing paraphysical experiences to take place where light-energy beings can make their appearance. The light phenomena can be experienced today, which we have done with various groups of people who share our meditation practice.

One of these locations we have used is Tulum which is a pyramid complex on the east coast of the Yucatan. Although the Yucatec Maya named it "wall," some say that it was originally called Zamá, or "the place of the dawning sun," perhaps a clue to the unique light phenomena associated with the ancient temple.

The largest pyramid within the complex is known as El Castillo, or "castle," and is where we gathered over 200 friends who were with us to activate the energies of this sacred site. In our guided meditation we visualized the Light of the Divine coming down upon the Castillo pyramid. To further activate this energy, we simultaneously created a powerful soundscape of resonance using seed syllables like *om-aum-umma*, which is Sanskrit-Arabic for "the eternal sound of unity," and *logos Theou*, which is Greek for "the word of God"; we also used some Egyptian, Hebrew, Aramaic, and Mayan expressions.

Some attendees saw a very strong light source, which surrounded Dr. J.J. Hurtak, and was briefly captured on film by a man photographing his wife. It appeared as an intense "energy shield" of superluminal light in response to our chanting of the ancient mantras. So powerful was the light burst of only a few seconds that some standing nearby shared momentarily feeling a shock from a powerful bolt of energy that almost knocked our translator off his feet.

In this case, the powerful light burst that we felt seemed to initiate a feeling of love that was very powerful, though brief. The ancients seemed to have wisely chosen Tulum's location for public celebration and prayer because the energies are still very strong there; it was an unusual energy that felt like the heavens were opening.

At Uxmal in the northwestern part of the Yucatan Peninsula, we later gathered a group of about 30 people within the sacred complex. It is one of many pyramidal sites south of the city of Merida, with the interesting large, oblong Pyramid of the Magician. According to legend, it was constructed in one day by a dwarf assisted by his mother, who was a shaman. The magician dwarf was said to have been hatched from an egg—and built the pyramid the following day.

That pyramid was probably first constructed between A.D. 600 and A.D. 1000, and the site includes a second "Great Pyramid," nunnery, ritual ball court, temple, governor's palace, and other buildings. Amid these structures that serve as a type of giant energy vortex being within special geomagnetic grid lines, we assembled to meditate and chant. In this guided meditation, we had participants visualize a spiritual "capstone" of energies atop the Pyramid of the Magician. Repeating the seed syllables and chanting Mayan and other sacred languages, it felt as if our bodies became a "tabernacle" of spiritual energy that followed the energetic design of the pyramidal form. We consider this chanting a calling out to higher energies, although in sacred sites, it is more of a realignment of ourselves to higher beings already operating in and around these vortex areas.

Within 10 minutes of chanting, many said they could feel the energy of a higher presence. And a light appeared, not physically in this case, but a paraphysical "light-event" was sensed by most of the group and captured live on video. The film revealed the light that remained for over three minutes, getting brighter over time. Even as the camera zoomed in on us as the group leaders, streams of white light clearly visible flowed down from above. There appears an overshadowing of white light above us on the film, as we sat and vocalized sacred sounds.

Imagine a higher communication system built into the sacred sites of the world; this is what we study, which is called archeo-acoustics. And we investigate how to tap into key sacred places like this that heighten human consciousness to a greater degree. The Great Pyramid in Egypt—and the one at Tikal, Guatemala, known as "the place of the voices or sounds"—are among others where we have documented similar light phenomena.

To create states that favor the building of a paraphysical energy field in a sacred area, we have developed the approach described above of forming a collective energy, using sacred geometry, guided meditation using sacred sounds, and breathing techniques. It mirrors what may have been meant by the figure of speech Christ used in the New Testament: that "even the stones will speak." The phrase carries profound musical and spiritual insights, into the sacred mathematical *gematria* or the linguistic structure of Divine harmonics that can be activated by people; they then become the living geometric "stones" or musical notes of a great temple of sound, participating in an acceleration of mental processes using the quantum or global mind as a blueprint for the next stage of evolution.

These sacred sites were not only designed to alter consciousness, but also to allow us to function as biotransducers and to connect to higher levels of consciousness. That is, in places like Uxmal, we sensed the presence of "higher beings." We obstruct our own capabilities of sensing them, while in our normal state of consciousness. The combined biomagnetic and psychomagnetic effects on our human nature can be enhanced, though, by deep meditation at a sacred site that is a geomagnetic gathering place for these untapped powers.

As to who or what is behind the light appearances, they could be true ancestors of these places, guardians who have watched over these sacred areas for generations. Usually these "light beings" appear simply as light, and often are just felt as a presence, although people sometimes receive some wisdom or insight, while others feel intense love vibrations associated with the light's appearance. However, the Mayan and pre-Mayan cultures performed ceremonies at these locations to ask for those "on the other side of the veil" to not only acknowledge the ritual, but to come and appear to them. Sometimes, there is a more detailed appearance, including a face. Therefore, the light can also be those from higher, superluminal realms, from higher dimensional realities understood by many as our greater ancestors.

The Mayan experience suggests these light beings are not a substitute for "The Source of All There Is." But their presence indicates that we are not alone in the universe, that there are many levels of intelligence connected with this planet, and that they wish to connect with us. Our experience is that we have nothing to fear from communing with these energies, as they represent our next phase of development, our "graduation" into a greater connection with a vast and awesome universe.

Drs. J.J. and Desiree Hurtak

CLAY AND CONSCIOUSNESS

I see her again, Allegra Topanga, a stunning goddess who dances with infectious joy as her long, flowing coils of brown hair, are in rhapsody with the breeze. As she graciously moves, her natural curves mirror the gorgeous mountainous landscapes surrounding her, while her feet reverently grace the earth, honoring its sanctity. The sun reflects off the turquoise jewel on her headdress, creating a radiant aura of light around her. The feathers in her hair blend with those of the large winged one perched on her shoulder. She commands the respect and admiration of all beings–the four-leggeds, two-leggeds, one-leggeds, for her alluringly captivating green eyes serve as a portal to Spirit.

Her poetic speech summons circles of beings to participate in an ecstatic yet prayerful chant, creating a circle of seekers eager to receive and embody the wisdom of the elders that channels through her vessel. She is a conduit of dynamic energy and a keeper of sacred stories. She heals all who know her.

I was blown away by this vision during a pottery class, as it had been almost three decades since Allegra Topanga had visited me. Little did I know then how deeply her return would impact every aspect of my life.

This majestic goddess had introduced herself to me when I was an anxious and quirky 13-year-old, questioning the organized religion I was being indoctrinated into, yet feeling inextricably connected to the entirety of the universe. Every time I stepped foot into nature, my "church," I heard the voices of the trees, rocks, and water; and fairies emerged who spoke to me in native tongues. As a child, I was as mesmerized as I was confused by her presence in a vision, as she appeared so familiar and so real. In fact, she felt like me from another lifetime, although the conditioning of my childhood called that belief into question.

Now, while sitting at a pottery workbench in an introductory class years later, I was in a spiritual healing crisis and quest to find my true self. And she appeared again. I immediately recognized her by the sparkling green eyes, tousled, wavy hair, and whimsical feathers and turquoise in the headdress. It was as if I had teleported back to a longed-for time and place, a place for which I didn't even realize I was homesick. Tears flowed as Allegra's energy moved through me.

I realized then that Allegra Topanga was the activation of my soul's past, my connection with lineages that had been forgotten, but were always with me. I spontaneously sketched her image on a crisp, white sheet of paper, even though I had barely the skill to draw a straight line. Even more astonishing was the beaming confidence that I would soon hand sculpt her into existence just as magically, though I had nothing more than Play-Doh experience under my belt.

Feeling my hands at work in the clay felt as old as time; and as my energy ecstatically cascaded with every intricately carved detail my fingertips created, my soul was resuscitated, and I was imbued with life. Nine months of dedicated work later, I created a piece of art that I could only have previously imagined in dreams. I was proud to bring to life this woman who had an energy, a purpose, a resonance, a song to sing, and a dance to dance. Allegra

Topanga: goddess of transformation, sacred storyteller, wisdom weaver, and medicine woman come to life by the work of my own two hands.

The reunion with her catalyzed my homecoming. I began hearing voices and songs and stories again, just as I had as a child; I had visions of the glorious lands upon which my feet once roamed alongside the wild buffalo; and I remembered the medicinal skills that had lain dormant within me. The land empowered me once again, activated my heart, and nourished my soul as I ventured out each day to connect with nature. My life became a continuous shamanic journey as my guides accompanied me as unwavering beacons of light who created a bridge between spirit and matter while I pursued the quest of soul remembrance.

As part of this renewal, each day I prayed: "Mother Earth, grant me the ability to find appreciation, fascination, and awe with the little things within the larger works of beauty you have created. Help me to align with the elements of Earth, to live in accordance with the seasons, and to trust in the natural order of things. In doing so, Mother Earth, I will live in communion with nature, with my ancestors, and light the way for future generations. And help me to shine light into my shadows to reveal all parts of me so that I can feel whole again. Help me remember my way home."

I gained added insight on next steps in a shamanic journey in which a panda and a black panther guided me to an opening in some brush where drums were scattered around the landscape as rock formations with trees growing out of them. *The answers you seek are in the drums*, my guides said. *Let them heal you. Let yourself heal them. Return to ceremony. Don't abandon the old. Go back to your roots.*

I listened. Drumming felt as familiar as riding a bike. Each time I played, I remembered past times of holding sacred ceremony around a fire, dancing, singing, and storytelling; I recalled days of walking through desert villages in the blazing sun and harvesting plants and talking to them while creating medicinal herb bundles.

With every beat made on the drums, I reconnected with the primal pulse of all of existence, and signs appeared everywhere. I had learned signs are about being open and ready to see the extraordinary in the ordinary. I was beginning to understand spiritual growth as a process of becoming our higher selves, the very essence of who we are. This loving, compassionate self holds the accumulated wisdom from all our lifetimes.

I began reframing my journey of personal development and healing as a quest of spiritual inquiry and evolution. Doing so amplified my growth and strengthened this higher connection, leading to more synchronicities, insights, and revelations. I was remembering myself home.

Intuitive hints about New Mexico continued until it became a joyful, relentless obsession. Drawn to Native American culture, I read and studied voraciously. I connected deeply in ceremony with shamanic teachers and medicine women, participated in online classes and watched videos about shamanic practices, animal communication, plant medicine, and sacred ceremony. Suddenly, the images, visions, and "feelings" from earlier in my life had a place to land. In my connections and communications with nature and the Earth, my knowledge of having been certain animals, obsession with the magical powers of long hair, and understanding the power of counterclockwise circles; now made sense.

Over time, journeying became an active form of meditation that supported creativity and a fiery imagination. To manifest anything in life, in a journey, I would ask my spirit guides specific questions or requests, such as, *What do I need to let go of?* or *Show me the way when I can't see one.*

In one such journey, I was guided by a panda to climb a high tree but was frightened and doubtful. A massive condor came and hooked his bright yellow-orange talons into my shoulders from behind, lifting me and flying upward. I eventually landed in a vast abyss of white light, where a guide tossed me a large purple marbled crystal sphere with the words "be hope for others" etched into it. I later identified that stone as a charoite, a rare and complex illuminating stone that is particularly important for healers.

By being consistent in my practices, I increasingly saw signs that reflected the meaning and messages received during journeys. Every aspect of life gradually became a magical metaphor. In turn, journeys became richer as I went deeper with greater intention.

In one journey, I sought to discover my true nature and how I could use it to serve. I saw myself as an older woman adorned in an ivory cloak with silver hair that touched the Earth. She held a wooden staff in her left hand and a large spherical charoite crystal in her right. As I watched, she gracefully walked to an open space and drew three large circles in the sand. Groups of people of all ages started walking toward her, organizing themselves around the circumference in a healing circle.

The woman stretched out her arms and wrapped them around everyone. Crouching down in the overlapping middle of the circles, she scooped up a handful of earth to form many clay bowls. As she offered each person a bowl along with a blessing, I was given the message that still guides me today: my role in this life is that of a wise elder who creates from the earth. Allegra Topanga was me, and I finally understood what my quest had been for.

Dr. Kristy M. Vanacore

TESHUVAH

*A*s I step into the ceremonial pool to immerse in the mikveh, I inhale a long breath and exhale even longer. It's uncomfortable to breathe in the small room that smells like what fire and brimstone must smell like if I believed in such a thing. But I smell flame and heat–not feel it. Fear and sulfur are what the smell brings to mind. Fiery pits of molten lava and people pulled under the water are what I expect to see in the tiled pool I'm in. But there is only a wisp of a hand slowly floating below the surface, just my hand disappearing instead.

As I prepare to immerse myself beneath this holy water for the first time in this ritual purification to be alone with my G-d, I see nothing and smell everything–I am scared. Stretching my hands out, I try to find the wall of the pool, anything to hold onto. My eyes serve no purpose in the darkened space. My hands and feet feel useless, there is no surface contact made.

I stick my tongue briefly into the water, needing to taste something, terrified of what might meet my open mouth. And then I hear the soft sound that resembles breathing—not like I breathe; it's an almost silent inhalation and then a loud exhalation that brings with it steam that rolls over my upper back and leaves behind an even stronger fire and brimstone smell in its wake.

An awareness of space, gone as I immerse myself in the water. I fear small spaces, and even worse, large spaces like the ocean where I cannot connect with anything. Nothing to grab. Nothing that will save me.

I consider my senses right now. I can definitely smell. I can barely hear and I can feel, though not touch anything physically yet. And where are my feet? I am determined to move forward, though, to take this first "step" of faith into the nothingness.

Go up, turn around and come back to me, I hear on flying breath. *Teshuva,* the voice continues in Hebrew in the sense of returning or renewal. But I don't understand the question.

Go up? Turn around? Where? I demand, physically disoriented. *Go up and turn around and come back to you?* I wonder.

I have trouble breathing and the sulfur smell and fear overwhelm me. I jump where I think up is and I suddenly feel my feet again. I am above the surface now. Staying long enough to turn slightly to the left, I gulp air before reluctantly going back under for the next immersion.

Opening my eyes underwater, I take in an expanse of beautiful blue water with many tiny boats on its surface. They are paper boats that are on fire, yet do not consume. These lit "lanterns" appear to float just above me, raining light down on me.

My vision shifts, and I feel my feet on sand as the water and the boats disappears from my sight. When I look down, I am in a long, white dress that moves with the wind. I feel safe here and want to stay in this beautiful liminality. There it is though–a slightly louder inhalation, and I steady myself for the shower of heavy mist and the smell of sulfur.

Go up. Turn around and return to me. Another command on the breeze, but my lungs feel fine and I feel safe.

I don't want to leave. *I don't want to leave.* I feel as though I am screaming out loud to the night sky, but I am not–they are merely words in my head. I am being pulled up as if in the middle of a tornado. Something then roughly turns me around and pushes me below the surface, with just enough time for a quick breath. I am standing in a torrential rain, where the cracking of lightning and smell of decaying flesh is strong. Somehow, the decaying flesh smell comes not through my nose. It is in my body, it is my body.

Crouching into myself, shaking from fear and the coldness of the rain, I brace myself against the wind. My feet have disappeared again.

"Stop," I whimper. "Please make this stop." I can hear myself speaking now. "Please stop."

Crying, I struggle to breathe. It's painful to breathe. One more moment and I will drown amid this great expanse of nothingness. I hear a hissing: *be careful what you demand next time and of who you demand it.* There was no soft request like the previous ones, no one asking to come back to them. Suddenly I am pushed down to my knees. So close to closing my eyes forever. *You are done here. Go.*

With this harsh send-off, I resurface, gasping for breath as I complete the third immersion. It is brighter now, and I notice that, if I do one more partial turn, I will again face the direction where I had started. One more turn. But where would the strength to go under the surface one more time come from?

Come back to me, I hear below the surface.

With a long exhalation and a deep breath, I am once more below the surface. I can feel my feet are moving in the water this time. I stretch my hands out as far as I can, unable to touch the walls, but knowing that they are there. I see every soul ever created, standing before me with their hands reaching out to me. They invite me into community. I feel fully seen and gently loved as I am held by each of them, as if I am back in my mother's womb and am being gently rocked to sleep by the sound of her heartbeat. But I realize that I cannot stay here much longer. My lungs have begun to strain against my chest.

As if the souls surrounding me sense that I must leave them, they open their hands, palms facing toward the surface, and gently lift their hands upward as I begin to float to the surface. I can go now. I have smelled the smells of hell, bathed in fire and light, been caught up in the center of nature's chaos and wrapped in the love of community. I am popping up out of the water with my head safely above the surface. My feet are now firmly on warm tiles, and my hands can feel the cool walls. I take a moment to adjust.

Once I can walk, I turn and unsteadily begin my pilgrimage out of the water and up the seven steps holding tightly to its railing. I count each step as I emerge. In front of me, a great white towel is being held wide by a woman averting her eyes. I look down and realize I am completely naked. Soft singing comes from the community outside of the door in front of me, and soft tears fall shamelessly from my eyes mixing with remnants of the waters I had just left behind me. As I am being wrapped up in this soft cloud of a towel, the attendant breathes into my ear: "*Mazel tov.*"

The singing outside the door is louder now and with my hand on the doorknob, I hesitate to leave this holy place. The singing persists. Realizing there is no longer any need to look back, that I had left what I needed to release in the water, I step through the door to the sounds of a welcome song and see the faces of my ancestors, of those I have always known.

"*Mazel Tov*, Yael. You are now Jewish. Welcome Home."

Rev. Yael Navid

THE TALL ONES

It was a chilly fall day when at an annual spiritual retreat I attended, I was stopped in the hallway by a colleague. Pulling me aside and holding my arm, she said, "Do you know about these tall people who stand next to you?"

"Yes," I said about these ancestors who are not like any others I'd experienced before, "I know about them."

My first experience came years ago in a hotel room in Barcelona, Spain, while attending the Parliament of the World's Religions. Awakened in the night and wondering if a burglar or hotel staff were in my room, I realized it was something else. I had a visitor. Somewhat used to etheric bodies and spirit visitors, I relax right away because, in these situations, you can only relax and see what is going to unfold.

Spirit visitors usually have no physical substance, but this one's garments become displaced when in contact with surfaces. It appears this visitor has mass, which is confirmed when the visitor comes and sits down on the bed. The visitor's skin is a striking translucent white, eyes are a blazing powder blue, and a height of perhaps eight or more feet tall, making it tight cornering not to hit something in the typical, rather small, European hotel room. But the vibrations emanated are of great love as if the visitor is holding the whole space in love.

The visitor starts communicating in a way that appears telepathic. *There is someone you need to find while you are here. Someone we need you to get a message to. I'm going to show you that person and I'm going to tell you some things about their past, so when you talk to them, they will take you seriously.*

An etheric picture of the face of the person I am to find appears clearly in front of me. We discuss what I am to tell the person about their past and the central message.

The person is an up-and-coming spiritual teacher, much dedicated to the unfolding of the Divine Feminine. But she does not know of the need to go to Turkey, which houses the vortex of the lineage of which she is a part. It is the lineage she is unknowingly being called to serve and experiencing that vortex directly, I am told, will provide her further direction and a deepening of her important work. The "where" in Turkey, and an incredible, resonant, transmissive form of love is shared with me from the riveting, blue-eyed visitor—who then is gone.

The next morning, I decide the best way to proceed is to visit the large square in front of the main building where the parliament is being held. Bingo. I quickly spot her and carefully approach, making sure she sees my Parliament IDs.

I explain the situation to her, including that I've been told she has been having some deep questions about the authenticity of her calling. I share the information and details about Turkey.

We see each other several times during the meeting's remaining days, and she is compelled to follow through. It is no surprise that fall when I receive a telephone call from her in Hawaii. After relaying many of the details of her successful experience in Turkey, I learn she is now continuing the work on the island, and all is going very well.

While the Barcelona visitor directly helped me help another healer, the following year, the "tall ones" helped a spiritual organization of which I'm a founding member. After several long chats with a close friend and one of the elder members, one night she calls me with an unusual request.

"Kurt, there is something we have not talked about. I don't know what it is, but there is something we have not talked about."

Meeting for supper, we reprise the oddness of the situation, and I suggest, "Why don't we just 'out' some things, some crazy things, and see if we stumble across whatever this is." I end up telling her about the incident in Barcelona and the "tall ones."

Her mouth drops open. "Yes, this is it," she says. "I think these are the ones a teacher wrote about in her journals. No one has ever been too sure about it. She was not sure if they were from some other place or even 'us' coming back from the future. But the message was always the same. 'Just keep doing what you're doing', 'just keep following these called paths.'"

We both go away satisfied, as another spiritual knowledge hole is mended.

A year later, as a guest of a spiritual teacher in the Dzogchen (Tibetan Buddhist) community, I attend their annual retreat. It is a silent retreat, and I am only dropping in on the meditations and chanting because, when listening to those chants, I can't stop crying. A person there seems quite uneasy and keeps coming and going, as if in quite a quandary. But I am staying to myself.

Resting in my room, I suddenly am in the company of a "tall one" who starts a much slower, very relaxed conversation compared to the Barcelona visitor.

Hum, the tall one says. *This person is also confused—not sure about their calling; not sure about what to believe. You need to tell them that these things happen; they need to wait and be confident... they need to feel sure that these things will clarify. Perhaps you can talk to them.*

Well, not so easy at a silent retreat. But I discover as the days elapse, a walking area that has been designated for attendees to meet and chat. *Why not just go out there and see if that person stumbles along?*

That afternoon, just 60 yards into a stroll along this garden path, the other person appears—obviously deep in thought and perhaps kicking a lot around in their soul. He is young—sincere—wondering. Approaching him, I recount his dilemma and the visitor's message. After a wonderful conversation, he tells me that this information is a godsend.

In another year, I fly to meet with the founder and head of a major organization and two colleagues. They are hoping to get advice on expanding their business from a younger, accomplished individual in their business arena, and are hoping I can arrange that. After a long plane flight and car ride, I arrive where we have decided to initially meet.

When I walk into the living area of this palatial place, *I must be in the right place* pops into my head; two "tall ones" are sitting in the room—waiting, it seems, with the very persons I have been invited to meet. The meeting begins with a long elaboration by my hosts of what has brought them to this turning point in their work. They are ready to make a big financial and physical move, investing in a new location and headquarters. They are two generations into their work. Can I make that introduction?

"Yes," I say, taking their presumably unknown company into consideration, "I can."

A day later we drive to another nearby city where I have arranged for them to meet this other leader, which goes well. The plan is blessed, and we retire to a restaurant for some supper and to relax. The cell phone of the trio rings, with the final asking price for the land they were considering.

"Do you want to buy the property?" the realtor asks.

"Yes," their leader says, and his wife breaks down in tears at the table as a long journey of uncertainty for them is finally over.

Who are these ancestors that share some of our physicality, but appear so different? The wise ones tell me they are part of our direct ancestry, direct lineage. And that sensing them has to do with affinity, spiritual availability, and being in an energetically uplifted place often related to a vortex.

A friend travels annually to a certain place that he says is the foundation for his calling. I asked him once, "Why do you go every year?"

"I meet someone there," he said, a tear in his eye.

Dr. Kurt Johnson

STAFF OF LIFE

n January 26, 2009, a potentially foreboding annular solar eclipse occurred along a slender passage starting in the South Atlantic Ocean, sweeping towards Africa and into the Indian Ocean. On this same day, my younger brother Michael Keola Jennings Morriss died in a freediving accident off the western coast of the Big Island of Hawai'i. Suffering from a shallow water blackout, my water-loving brother drowned and lost his life at 23 years old.

When my sister told me the news over the phone, I threw all social niceties out the window, screaming helplessly into the shadowy air in my small San Francisco apartment until no more sound came out. As I returned home to the Big Island of Hawai'i, reality hit home, as well. A light in my world was gone. My family's close-knit community was aghast. Our radiant Michael Keola–meaning "staff of life" in Hawaiian–would no longer walk among us. His staff of life had burned out—or so it seemed.

After sleeping on the floor in my sister's room for a month, it was time to give her space and move into my brother Michael's room. Glancing at his painfully worn down, navy-blue crocs, whose position remained unchanged on the floor, I hurt to the depths of my soul. Michael was the last thing I thought about each night, as headlights from cars speeding along Kawaihae Road flickered into the second-story room, their sounds slowly fading into the dewy, Waimea darkness.

One night, I was jolted awake. I could feel the bed beneath me, but when I tried to move my body in the dimly lit room, my legs and arms were paralyzed, as if cemented to the bed itself. Confused and concerned, I somehow knew despite my fluttering thoughts that reality had radically shifted.

Everything happened so quickly, I didn't have time to consider whether I was awake or dreaming or somewhere in between. A brilliant white light was radiating out of the center of the room, and quickly filled all but its far edges. The light had rays tinged with a brilliant yellow-silver color. It was an exquisite, glimmering, ethereal substance.

In my heart, mind, and soul–my integrated consciousness–I knew the light was Michael. I was as certain of that as the feeling of wetness you get the moment you dive into the ocean. It was a knowing so simple and effortless that it rang as truth.

I communed in total presence with the moment, without awe, disbelief, joy, or grief. In that span of time, an experience as pure as the light that had overtaken the room overtook me. It is what I imagine it would feel like to be in the presence of a fully enlightened master.

Within the dispersed, radiant glow, a much smaller, denser light slowly moved the focus of the light in the room. The bright silver, sparkling ball shimmied a bit, like light moving across the sea; not quite in a straight line, but had grace, nonetheless. The ball glided in front of my savasana positioned body moving toward my left hand. It "touched" the center of my left palm, the way wind kisses *hāpu'u*, Hawaiian tree ferns; contact is made with their leaves, yet no visible trace of the interaction remains.

The brilliant orb infused pure light into my left palm, which returned to its natural state in an instant after the caress. The glowing ball effortlessly glided above my body toward my right palm, and Michael imbued my right hand with light.

Awakening hours later to a room filled with daylight I packed the experience away in my short-term memory. A day or two later, I had my weekly therapy session over the phone with my therapist and shared my deep anguish about Michael's empty blue crocs, still in the same kapakahi (crooked) position. I was haunted by the absence of his feet, yet unable to cry. She confirmed my desolate revelation, which made me feel worse. When I described the strange dream I had about Michael the prior evening, she gently yet emphatically said, "Lindsey, that was not a dream, that was a visitation."

I explained that hands reminded me of reiki, of energy healing, of the power to heal others, and to pass on transmissions of rejuvenation, restoration, and light. Hands meant getting out of the mind and intellect and into the body, the spirit, the energy realms, and beyond.

It took several moments–and years, ultimately–for Michael's visitation to fully sink in. My sweet and fiery Michael may have entered his deepest meditation state in the depths of the waters. In his zen spot off the Big Island's west coast, he had traded in his earth body and let his spirit dance. Now I know that in his light body, he dives through dimensions beyond what I can typically see, a radiant expression of the beyond. I can now recall his light and be bathed in both mystical awe and sweet relief. For our staff of life has become a guiding staff of light.

Lindsey Uluwehimailani Morriss

MEETING AT SERPENT MOUND

*Y*ou never know where your past may meet you, as I was reminded after being asked to perform a ceremony at the Serpent Mound in Ohio. Thousands of years ago, Native Americans had created the mound in the shape of a snake with a curled tail and other massive earthworks, such as nearby burial mounds. Serpent Mound is now a National Historic Landmark overseen by Ohio's parks department, which had invited me there to lead an equinox ceremony.

While on the phone about the request from the parks department, an invisible being spoke to me.

I'm here. I can hear you, I communicated.

Flordemayo, ask if you could stay on the land, the holy one said to me.

When the gentleman on the other end of the line asked if I had any questions, I said, "Can I stay overnight? Can I stay on the land? Can I be there with the serpent that night?"

"Oh, Grandma Flordemayo, this is a national park," was his response "We don't allow anyone to stay. We have the parks keepers, but we don't allow the public to come in and stay overnight."

My silence led him to ask if I would still come otherwise.

"No. I cannot come," I said, and explained the reason: "Because the holy being is speaking to me right now and the holy one is telling me to stay on the land. And if I don't have permission to stay on the land, I will not come."

"Grandmother, let me call you back," he said.

When he called back, he said they would provide a sleeping area for me overnight. And so, I agreed.

I shared the information of my visit and about 500 people came for the ceremony from as far north as Canada, and as far south as Florida. It lasted a whole day, with a prayer fire ceremony, chanting, and drumming. At five o'clock I did as instructed by the parks department and was the first one to "leave" so that others did not think about staying. I made a big exit, saying goodbye to everybody and making sure they saw me leave. Staff closed the park, and then invited me and another to come back to stay overnight, while they provided guards for us.

Park staff had set me up with a little cot and a tent; but of course, I wanted to be outside the whole night. We were in an area that's very close to the serpent's head, perhaps on the shoulder of the serpent. From there, you could see a beautiful egg that she carries in her mouth.

Looking at the heavens while we prayed, a dear friend sang and played a sacred, metal drum-like instrument called a *hong*.

I witnessed incredible orbs of light. It was like we were being showered by the beautiful light coming in from the heavens. Then a grandmother materialized next to me on the right side, sitting in a very small rocking chair. I was aware that grandmother did not seem as though she was supposed to be there.

I turned and looked at her, saying, "Grandmother, where did you come from?" Then I stood up from where I was to be face to face with the grandmother, repeating the question.

"Child, I've come to tell you that I am of your mom's people," she replied.

I got a little closer to the grandmother to see her features, saying to myself, *My mom's people. Does the grandmother have the familiar face, the familiar nose, mouth, eyes that my mother, my grandmother have?*

As I got really, really close, she said, "It is your mom's people that built these mounds."

"Grandmother, I'm the first generation that has traveled into these mountains. I'm the first generation that is here in this United States. I don't know of my grandmother's people being here."

"Child, I assure you that your people built these mounds."

By then, I had gotten very close to the grandmother and realized that she was not breathing. Her chest was not moving up and down. As soon as I realized that she disappeared.

The essence, the spirit, the light of the grandmother was now all within me. After I came home, my husband asked if I was all right, and I replied "no," and explained my experience. I became very emotional doing so, because I could feel the grandmother just moving throughout my body.

"Is there any way that I could find out through my DNA if I'm related to the people in Ohio?" Saying the word Ohio, even, felt very foreign to me then.

Before I knew it, I received my test results that showed 2,000 years ago, my grandmother's people were in the Ohio area. They then came back into Central America, traveled as far south as Colombia, South America, and returned to Central America.

I have been very touched by this knowledge. Pay attention to your attraction to sacred sites and places. You may not know the root of that connection, but in ancestral times, you, as your elders, may have stood in that sacred site to offer ceremony and prayer, and now you have an opportunity to receive all that energy back.

Grandmother Flordemayo

HEALING AND THE ANCESTRAL BRIDGE

"Everything is going to be alright," the medicine man whispered in my ear.

I was attending an intensive mind-body medicine training in Boulder, Colorado and on this day, we went to a Native American lodge up in the mountains. We spent the day learning from an Indigenous medicine man from a local tribe. After a morning of teaching and speaking, he intuitively picked two people from the group to do a healing ceremony. I was selected. I had had a hysterectomy years earlier, and I was consciously working to heal some second chakra energetic and emotional patterns of trauma. The other person he chose had a brain tumor. Before selecting us, the medicine man knew nothing of our personal lives or health histories.

He proceeded to work nonverbally, with us standing within the Medicine Wheel he'd created. While other members of his tribe were drumming and chanting, he danced and chanted to the rhythmic beat, moving purposefully and magically, focusing on my second chakra region and my fellow student's head. The healing ceremony intertwined between the two of us, simultaneously focusing on one, moving to the next, and back again. All the other members of our training group sat in a circle around the room and observed. It was a sacred, deeply moving experience.

Later that night, I had an optional individual-healing session scheduled with an energy practitioner, who was teaching a segment of the intensive. She had developed her own hybrid process of intuitive energy healing. She started by invoking her spiritual guides, Mother Mary and Mary Magdalene. Then, pausing to ask whether I would like to invoke the presence of any deity in prayer, she continued to call in several other masters and guides.

She began sweeping her hands in broad strokes over my body, specifically over the chakras, to release what she referred to as energy blockages and emotional residue. She asked me to participate and pay attention to any signs, symbols, feelings, or sensations I might have as she moved across my body. It was her intention to follow my energy as the different cues directed the flow and healing process.

As she was working on my second chakra region, I felt a profound shift. My body began to surge through an extreme metamorphic process of twists and contortions. I couldn't control the movements. My hands curled up like those of my grandmother, who had severe rheumatoid arthritis, and my limbs and torso displayed broad sweeping movements like someone with cerebral palsy. I tried to communicate to the healer what I was experiencing, but I couldn't speak. My mouth and face were captured in the same involuntary, palsied process. She knew. Trying to reassure me that everything was okay, she continued to work with the energy around my body, sweeping and holding the field as I was forced to surrender deeper into the experience.

Suddenly, the transpersonal realm opened. The room was transformed— luminous—and I could hear the drums and chanting from the earlier ceremony with the medicine man. The drumming was comforting, like an ancestral lullaby soothing my anxious mind. All the while, I still couldn't speak, and I couldn't control my body.

Gradually, the room disappeared as the space filled with women—my ancestors. Generation after generation of women became visible off to my left, presenting as an inverted triangle. Dressed in drab and modest pioneer-type clothing, these multitudes of women appeared to span for miles. Off to my right felt like an abyss of unmanifested, pure, potential Source energy; the unborn and future generations of women held by the Divine Feminine.

A Divine feminine presence was in the room, and I deeply felt the feminine presence extending her gratitude toward me. I also felt the gratitude of all the women looking toward me from the left corner. In a flash, another dimension opened. I was shown how healing the feminine wound on the planet for the present generation was connected to healing the wounds of past and future generations. In that moment, my own personal healing was woven into the integral web of life.

The same Divine Source that connects all things was using this experience to teach me the importance of reconciliation across generations as the past, present, and future all exist in that infinite flowing presence of now. There is no separation. I became the ancestral bridge.

When the twisting and contorting stopped, my body slowly unwound itself and softened into a relaxed but extremely fatigued state, feeling as if I had run a marathon or given birth to a baby.

"Did you hear the drumming?"

Those five words the healer said were powerful and redemptive. She had heard the drumming and had witnessed an element of the multidimensional experience. We'd had the experience together.

The two separate healing sessions of the day had merged into one profound experience that crossed all boundaries of time and space. Simultaneity had come about between my own personal healing and that of the planet and generations of ancestral women. I was given new information and instructions—shown new layers of the cosmic template.

That day, there was a palpable connection between my two healers, the field, the ancestors, and myself. With no dialogue or medical history, both healers tapped into the mystery of the universe and *knew* exactly what was needed. Their connection to Source/Great Spirit yielded perceptive intuition and guided a radical healing experience.

Through this experience, another significant gateway had presented itself. In over thirty years of profound mystical experiences, I had never intimately shared a multidimensional experience with another credible, witnessing adult. Now for the first time, the thin veil between heaven and earth lifted and another person had a simultaneous mystical experience of another realm with me.

None of it could make sense to a linear-thinking, logical, rational mind that is informed by only five senses. And that is okay. The experience didn't have to make sense. I left with a profound sense of grace, deep healing, and a tender new connection with my ancestors.

Dr. Julie Krull

THE VALLEY OF THE ANCESTORS

*T*he North Crestone Creek Trail begins in a beautiful forest in the Sangre de Cristo Mountains. Sitting on a rock next to the creek to enjoy the surroundings, I began my morning meditation. An uncomfortable sensation soon arose, and I felt assaulted by something invisible that was trying to get my attention. Tuning in, I realized that I was being fired upon with etheric arrows. Each strike to my chest brought a sting of external anger to my emotional body. The Native American guardian spirits of the land were shooting at me.

Clearly, I had somehow provoked their anger, yet I had barely entered the forest. Their arrows conveyed a sense of trespassing, making me wonder if other hikers were sensitive enough to notice, or I was being targeted for being sensitive enough to get the message. Either way, I needed to appease these spirits before moving forward.

Rather than be perceived as just another non-native trespasser on their sacred land, I wanted to respect their guardianship and ask permission as a visitor. So, I thanked the spirits telepathically for their presence, acknowledged their anger and their relationship to the land, and asked for permission to respectfully enter the sacred forest. Immediately, the arrows stopped, and we started an interaction based on mutual listening. They conveyed to me that, after many of them had passed into the dreamtime, they had vowed to remain with the land as sacred guardians until new guardians arose that could accept that responsibility. I felt touched by their plight and stewardship as ancestor guardians waiting patiently to impart their secrets.

A deeper focus of listening came over me, informed by the powers of listening the native spirits practiced, which attuned my inner senses. In the silence that followed the exchange, I entered a deeper meditation state, hearing only the wind rustling through the trees, and the babbling creek flowing past me. Suddenly, the trickling water sound shifted, becoming like a conversation. I began to hear the communications of the nature spirits in the form of a water language.

Once my senses became attuned to their language, the spirits took notice of me. *He can hear us!* I heard them say.

A bridge with the realm of the invisible nature spirits opened to me, the deeper listening practices of the Native American guardians began transferring to me. It was a turning point in a long journey of integration with this other reality that opened many new doors of perception.

Hiking up the trail, I had quite the entourage following in the spirit world. The native guardians continued working with me, as the nature spirits tuned into my thoughts, curious about this person who was finally listening to them. My mind drifted at one point, and a Beatles song became stuck in my head.

What is the purpose of this song? they said.

It was a curious question, revealing the contrast between our realities. I veered off the trail and found a rock to sit against while meditating and practicing the art of listening to these nature spirits.

Surrounded by the indescribably beautiful forest, I sat quietly and heard the creek in the distance, while taking in the valley below filled with Aspen trees. I felt a group of nature spirits hovering in front of me, and we started to commune more deeply. I explained that the song was meant to celebrate life and human love.

They seemed to understand but shared a totally different take on the purpose of singing when asked. *We sing to help the plants and trees grow.*

With that, my mind became flooded with the awareness that they created subtle sounds and vibrations with their thoughts to help nurture, to heal, and to even sculpt the natural landscape. These beings were builders of natural form.

Aware that this interaction was just the tip of the iceberg, I vowed to humble myself more regularly, knowing how much the secrets of the land and communing with the invisible guardians were worth. I became more alert from then on for signs of how to continue this inner dialogue.

My dreamtime connections with the ancestors also deepened. At one point, a Native American guardian spirit of the sacred valley revealed himself directly to me. In the dream, I was sitting under the stars in the San Luis Valley while he performed a ceremony with me. He spoke prayers in a native tongue and blew tobacco smoke over my shoulders. The intention was to bless the link that was developing between myself as a channel and other worlds, a connection the ancestors had worked to anchor into the land.

The San Luis Valley was once called the "Bloodless Valley" by the Navaho. The Native American tribes that visited there then had long practiced setting aside their weapons and treating this land as a shared place of spiritual pilgrimage.

The far-reaching value of this place became apparent while attending an experiential workshop. The facilitator invited the participants to say a prayer, so that all our ancestors would benefit from the inner work. A terrible, heavy feeling overwhelmed me, reminiscent of the arrows of anger on North Crestone Creek Trail. One after another, my ancestors began heaping their pains and unresolved energies onto me for healing. Tormented, I considered how to develop a buffer, some system that would allow maintaining integrity with my own mood and vibrancy.

As I sat there, I commanded, "Let there be a valley under the stars where ancestors can only come to meet me in the presence of a Violet Flame bonfire."

I began to imagine a place in the dreamtime that could act as a meeting space for this work. It seemed time to bring forth the spirit of the Bloodless Valley to do healing work for a new age. The next time I sat down to continue the visualization, I was delighted by how well the process worked. I meditated and focused on the Valley of the Ancestors, visualizing this sacred place under the stars. As I found my focus on the Violet Flame bonfire, I imagined placing my bare feet on the earth and approaching the fire while inviting any ancestors who wanted to work with me to meet me at the Violet Flame. I could feel many of their spirits gather around.

Both the Native Americans and white settlers in my genetic lineage had unique woes, but often had unresolved energy toward each other. My commitment to holding equal space for the resonance of all these lineages turned out to be key to unlocking the ceremony's potential.

The Violet Flame directed me to begin stepping into the energetic positions of each of the ancestors gathered around the fire, as if stepping into their shoes. Each time I did this with feeling, I gained a new perspective, while seeking to undo that which impeded the vibration of wholeness within them as one spirit. I was spontaneously guided to use the Hawaiian *Ho'oponopono* prayer: I'm sorry. Please forgive me. Thank you. I love you.

I began saying this at each position that I stepped into, allowing those who wanted to do so to speak its words through my voice. I also began to listen for those who instead needed to receive this prayer to enter a new spiral of forgiveness. The openness of the ceremonial approach allowed what needed to happen to become clear, so that everyone who felt called to contribute was guided into their roles.

My heart expanded tremendously as I felt the power of this simple ceremony overcoming all cultural and language barriers that had prevented ancient tribes and settlers from speaking a common language of peace. I hope one day, we will walk as the new guardians and stewards of the land, entrusted with the secrets of our beloved Mother Gaia. And that the restless spirits that have remained in waiting for us to do this can be released to journey on, their sacred purpose on earth fulfilled.

Saryon Michael White

FAMILY CONTACT

I shared a room with my sister for many years. At bedtime, my sister had a habit of passing out quickly, but this night, I heard movement and felt her physically sit on my bed while I was facing toward the wall. Turning over to ask what she needed, I saw an empty spot and that she was fast asleep across the way. I somehow knew it was my maternal grandfather who passed on my birthday when I was six years old.

For Easter that year, we did our annual egg hunt in our front yard and grandfather had a surprise for me. We were close in spirit, and he appeared in many childhood dreams. That night in my dreams, he showed me that I had missed a hidden egg and where it was located. The next morning, I dragged my older sister outside despite the rain to find this tiny chocolate egg; it was right next to the rock where he had shown me it would be.

My paternal grandfather also liked to make his presence known in our house, especially late at night, when he could be heard climbing up the stairs. He would go to each bedroom to check on his grandchildren. And one night in a dream, before my dad passed, my grandfather visited me with my aunt. I was walking on a pier into the ocean when he appeared, but he was, surprisingly, very young. My aunt refused to look at me, as if afraid to tell me something.

The dream startled me awake. They were coming to take my father "home" and awoke me to remember that message. My father had a long list of health problems, and we were very close and spent much time together. I told him about the dream. Unsurprised, he shared that he expected to be passing very soon, possibly in winter.

However, we had received something of a reprieve. Dad had an accident the summer before he passed away, after jumping into my brother's pool. He had blacked out, and said it was like a switch went off inside: he couldn't move, swim, or breathe, and was just sinking to the pool's bottom. My brother dove in and saved him. Meanwhile, our neighbor's father drowned in a pool accident the same day.

Dad spent a lot of time after that in a hospital, as his lungs kept filling with fluid that his heart just could not pump out. He told me in a dream later that he was supposed to die during the pool incident but was given four extra months because a hurricane was coming that would flood our town. My mom could not have handled the combined grief of losing him and the flooding.

The borrowed time was filled with hospital visits and poor health for Dad. When he passed, I heard him from the other side almost immediately. A phone call from my mother came at 4 o'clock in the morning that he had died in his sleep. While driving over to say goodbye, his voice boomed inside my car. His message was that this grief could sink me, could drown me, or I could swim through it and ride it out. He reminded me that he'd taught me how to swim and said that was what he wanted for me—to just keep swimming.

I experienced a deep grief, but through music and other outreach, my dad helped me overcome it. He had played the saxophone when he was younger and had been in a band. All six siblings grew up playing an instrument or singing, so music was a big part of our life. So he would visit my bedside and sing songs. Sometimes they were more about a message in the lyrics than being meaningful to him while alive. Although Dad definitely was not a Coldplay fan, he would sing "Yellow" to me to explain that where he was, there was a golden light. Or he revisited his big band and Doo Wop roots by singing "Tears on My Pillow" by Little Anthony and The Imperials to share that he saw my tears from grieving his death.

I soon moved back home to help my mother out after his death, but also knew that his presence would be stronger there. He started connecting by "tapping" the top of the garbage can and making it rock. He'd done the same thing while alive in the dining room. But Dad did it so often that Mom tried to squelch it by buying an electric waste basket. Only, she had to remove the batteries a couple of days later as electronics turned out to be easier for spirits to maneuver.

Another night, he came to my bed as an apparition who had to take me somewhere. I felt my soul lift away from my body and could see my body still in the bed. There he stood, and I asked, "Dad, where do we have to go?"

"The Pleaides," he answered and smiled. I didn't understand what he meant at the time.

We walked down the hallway steps and our souls passed through an antique mirror that my mom kept in the downstairs hallway. I felt the sensation of flying before our landing in a place made of glass and crystal. I walked down some crystal steps to find a beautiful woman below.

"Welcome home" she said, handing me a calla lily in what appeared to be a party setting. I saw souls that were bluish in color, with peacock feathers on their head and back.

My dad shared that this is my home on the other side. That we all envision heaven as a resting place, or a garden, which are options, but that it is more about having a place where the departed decompress from human life and review all the things we had done, good and bad. After doing so, we return to the star systems.

He said that he is currently in the Andromeda galaxy, but wanted to show me my future home, and why I had always felt different from others as an empath with heightened clairvoyant senses. He also said that our star families can help guide us, if we ask for assistance. The message received, I crashed back into my human body.

Awakening the next morning, I was exhausted, as if I had not slept at all. To help me accept the lesson, he came again and showed me what I look like when I'm in my heaven, and what his spirit self looks like as well—both very different than our human forms.

The visits over the years have sometimes come in dreams or when I'm driving and hear his voice, such as asking me to buy my mom roses for their anniversary. After I brushed him off, he came back and reminded me. My mom was so happy with the dozen red roses, and we laughed at Dad bugging me until I bought them.

I'm so blessed that through thick and thin, my family's ancestors pop in to cheer me on and help me out.

Ginny Colarusso

FLY FREE

*M*y miracle trip to Italy had come to an end. Having played baseball and softball my entire life, it was an opportunity of a lifetime after college to play softball in Macerata, Italy. When the season ended, I was returning home proud and ready to share my experience with my Italian grandmother, Nonni, who lived next door to us.

After an eight-hour flight from Rome to New York, another to my home state, and then a two-hour drive, I was tired but excited to see family. With hellos said to my sisters, I hurried next door, heart pounding with excitement to see my Nonni, a dearly loved and loving part of our immediate family.

While I was away Nonni had been diagnosed with cancer. My heart sank into the pit of my stomach, horrified to see only a fraction of the woman she had been. She had begun chemotherapy and radiation treatment while my season was wrapping up, and her big smile seemed bigger because her body was so diminished now. I did my best to hold back tears of devastation, my excitement replaced with guilt for going overseas, and guilt for not coming back sooner; along with sadness and then anger for the time that I had lost with her.

My parents encouraged me to tell tales of my European adventure to help liven the mood. I did so while sharing treasures, photos, and newspaper articles. I had even brought back a friend who stayed for 10 days and was a delightful diversion for us all.

However, once she departed, the stark reality and immense load of sharing the responsibility with my mother of caring for Nonni set in. I'd deliver soup and sit by Nonni's bedside, recalling places I had visited in Italy and heroics on the softball field when she was awake. She always championed my sports endeavors, despite not understanding much about the games. I also accompanied her to doctor visits and treatment days and was there for the following days of sickness that resulted.

In February, I received a call from my coach in Macerata about returning to play a second season. It felt like a no-brainer, and my parents were supportive. I could see that the news gave them a boost as they asked many questions: Would I live in the same place, and have a roommate? Would I get a moped? When would the season start, and when would I be leaving?

I sidled up beside my grandmother afterward to watch television with her. She was now living with us in a room just off the dining room. She asked me to turn the volume down, which surprised me because it was a favorite show of hers, starring Angela Lansbury.

Her voice weak, Nonni motioned with a finger for me to lean closer. "I heard that you are thinking of going back to Italy."

"Well, they have asked me to go back to play again. I haven't thought about it yet," I responded sheepishly.

"I wish you wouldn't go," she whispered. "I like your company."

Nodding, I took her hand in mine. My Nonni had never once left me feeling disappointed about anything. An uplifting person and a giver, she always made everything feel better. It was decided.

The next day, I waited six hours to accommodate the time difference and called my coach in Italy, Franco. "Mi dispiace (I'm sorry), but I cannot return to play this season," I said steadfastly. He agreed to stay in touch and let me know how the team was doing.

As my grandmother's plight worsened and the daily routine became more burdensome, my mother encouraged me to visit my college friends for a weekend to have some fun. It was hard to leave her to manage everything but even harder to continually watch my mother's heart break a little more each day. When I returned, mom wearily asked me to try to get Nonni to eat some soup she'd prepared.

"She needs to eat. The doctor said she needs to eat," she said with desperation.

I took the soup to my grandmother and playfully tried to get her to take a few spoonfuls.

"You eat it for me. Please eat it," Nonni implored.

I froze, as I couldn't bear the thought of what it meant for me to eat that soup. I did not want to eat it or let her go. I wanted to demand like my mother that she eat it. My heart aching inside me, without taking a breath, I took a spoonful of soup and swallowed.

My Nonni patted my knee and closed her eyes.

Over the next 48 hours, family gathered to take turns at her bedside and at comforting each other. The bravest shared heartfelt stories, and some tearfully shared, "I love you." The days that followed were filled with the rituals and ceremonies that go with someone's passing. Returning home after the funeral, the house gradually filled to capacity and became disturbingly lively—even boisterous. It felt as if no one was honoring my sadness.

I sat in an angry trance. My uncle called out to me from another room startling me; people were looking for me and saying, "telephone." I didn't move.

My uncle made his way to me through the crowded space to share that, "The airline called and said your pre-paid tickets to Italy are ready for you."

I was perplexed by the message. I had told Franco that I wasn't returning, but he had gone ahead and made the arrangements anyway. On the flight to Rome a few weeks after laying my grandmother to rest, I looked out among the clouds and said, "Thank you Nonni."

Immediately I felt shivers travel down my entire body. Moments later I understood when I noticed the woman sitting next to me had a magazine open to a page with a picture of Angela Lansbury.

Chris Ciepiela

ANCESTRAL TROOPS IN WALES

*D*eep in the heart of the Brecon Beacons National Park in Wales in the remote hamlet of Talybont-on-Usk, population 743, I arrive in a place where I have never been before but to which I am inherently connected.

Drenched and lugging a suitcase, I enter the dining room of my B&B where locals are finishing their Sunday roast dinner. It is pouring outside, and I have no umbrella or raincoat. The host shuffles me to a table in front of the open hearth and pours me a glass of sherry.

"You'll warm up quickly here," she says, and I know I have come to the right place.

Even though I'm a world traveler, I realize I am ill-prepared for this journey. Like a myotonic goat, I feel my body could seize up, tipping over at the slightest scare. I hope the two gentlemen and lovely lady lunching next to me don't notice I'm teetering on the edge. They are eyeing me, and I'm sure wondering what an American female is doing alone so far from home. But I am not a tourist. I'm on an ancestral journey, and it is both deeply personal and necessary.

Since the dismantling of my own childhood home at the young age of eighteen, I have been bouncing around the globe trying to root in foreign soil in Europe, Asia, the Middle East, and for the last decade, Central America. I'd even fooled myself into believing I had finally found "home" in Costa Rica. But then a metaphorical fire raged, and overnight, everything I loved was gone-my home, my job, my man, and worse … my sense of belonging. Now, completely untethered at the age of fifty-five, my need to unearth my ancestral past to give meaning and connectedness to my life has become imperative.

My quest to walk in the footsteps of my forefathers was inspired, in part, by years of online genealogical research. DNA testing from my 88-year-old father linked his paternal lineage back to Sir Roger Vaughan, and our interest escalated. Vaughan had fought alongside his legendary father-in-law, Dafydd Gam, in the Battle of Agincourt in 1415. They lost their lives on French soil to save King Henry V. From Vaughan, our Welsh line descends 300 years to the Vaughans of Tretower Court and Castle, who were movers and shakers among the landed gentry during the Tudor years.

The descendants of Tretower include Henry Vaughan, poet and doctor, and his twin brother, Thomas, a priest and alchemist. Both left a mark on seventeenth-century literature, with Henry recognized as a great confessional, visionary poet who influenced Wordsworth and other poets who followed.

A love of poetry is in our DNA. My father often cries when reciting poems, so it seems appropriate to begin my ancestral journey here along the shores of the River Usk—inspiration for much of the Vaughan twins' work. I want to give my father the knowledge of his ancestral past before he departs. But mostly, I need to know if my ancestral spirits are with me; and that somehow, I am not alone.

While in Cardiff just days before, the magnitude of my newfound solitary journey had overwhelmed me. I had taken solace in an old church. Sitting in a pew, I immediately began crying. *What did I hope to find tromping around centuries-old cemeteries and villages? And what was I going to do now that I had no sense of belonging to anyone or anywhere?*

Cocooned in the chrysalis of those ancient church walls; a metamorphosis took place. My consciousness shifted to another dimension, one that felt in connection with the spirit world. And I heard myself call out, "all my relations, all my relations, all my relations!"

The first time I had ever heard someone invoke the spirits of their ancestors was back in my thirties. I attended a Native American sweat lodge ceremony in the backwoods of Georgia. A Lakota Chief had heated lava stones and transferred them inside a domed, willow branch-and-tarp structure, pouring water on the stones to create steam. Tobacco and sweetgrass were added to purify and balance our minds, bodies, and spirits. We repeated the chant "all my relations," summoning the "ancestral troops" to assist in our healing and transformation.

Throughout my journey in Wales, I would find myself repeating this chant, silently at first, but then out loud with proud intention, whenever entering places where I believed my ancestors had roamed: churches, cemeteries, castle ruins, even pubs.

I finish my pork and parsnips by the open fire at my B&B and contemplate an afternoon nap. Preparing to leave, the jolly-faced gentleman at the next table stops me.

"You're an American, are you?" he asks, obviously having heard my accent.

"Yes, from Oklahoma."

After the typical half-sung reference to the Oklahoma musical's lyrics about "wind sweepin' down the plain," I quickly explain my focus and intention to walk the Henry Vaughan Walk, a scenic stroll along the Monmouthshire and Brecon Canal that includes wooden signposts with extracts of the Vaughan's poetry.

The man introduces himself as Malcolm. Next to him, the formerly talkative gentleman dressed in his Sunday best but with a few Pimms in, falls silent.

"I'm a descendant of Henry Vaughan," he states, rising to his feet.

We stare at each other, mystified. Tears come to our eyes as we realize we are in the presence of family. We embrace like long-lost cousins.

Colin Jones Vaughan, as he calls himself, insists I join their table. I learn that every Sunday, these joshing and jesting "Three Musketeers" meet for verbal swordplay aimed at cheering each other up. I discover that Jane and the men are each recovering from their own metaphorical fires. Each has lost a loved one, cementing our bond.

Malcolm declares, "We must take this child immediately to the cathedral!"

The three nod as if going to church were quite urgent. They discuss the proper hour to enter.

"Timing is everything," Colin whispers.

It's decided to first visit Colin's house to compare genealogical records; then we'll stop by Jane's for her camera and head to Malcolm's. To my great fortune, Malcolm is also a local historian with a wealth of information about the Vaughans of Breconshire. I feel as if my ancestors have helped me stumble upon this perfect trio to lead me on an adventure into the land of my forefathers.

"Malcolm has a key," Colin says while winking, and I know we're in for trouble.

Although I wouldn't normally run off with two men I didn't know to their homes, or worse, church, there was something about Jane and her funny, googly-eyed sheep socks and penchant for the profane that made me trust the lot of them. I only hoped the mischievous trio wasn't planning some sort of forced repentance for past Vaughan family sins.

Like D'Artagnan of *The Three Musketeers*, I enter the gates of Brecon Cathedral behind my escorts and am transfixed. Christians have worshiped here for more than a thousand years, from the days of the Celtic Church, even before the Norman Conquest. My spine tingles considering my ancestors most certainly worshiped here too. We stop briefly under an enormous oak to pay tribute to my new friends' loved ones buried here. But daylight is fading.

"Quickly, we must go inside," Malcolm says, turning the skeleton key.

Malcolm has a flashlight for the dim insides and hurries us to a door leading to a narrow, winding staircase.

"Watch your heads," he adds as we head up to the bell tower, stopping just beneath it. "Look through there," Malcolm instructs.

I peer through a narrow slit in the stone wall to the sanctuary below. The sunlight streams through the stained-glass window and I see my ancestor, Sir Roger Vaughan, draped in full kaleidoscopic color. And in the foyer stands a stone carving of my other famed ancestor, Henry Vaughan—doctor, poet, mystic. Our timing could not have been better!

Back in the car, Colin insists on stopping again at his home. He gives me an oversized green raincoat of his twin brother, who had died years before. His eyes soften as he drapes the Mackintosh over my shoulders.

"It's a little big for you, but it will protect you on your walk tomorrow."

The next morning, it is indeed pouring. I awake with the discouraging realization that everything I have held dear is gone and consider disappearing back beneath the covers. But I have come for the Vaughan Walk and walk I will.

Pulling the rubber hood of my new Mackintosh over my head, I shove my hands into its mammoth pockets and head out along the narrow canal, the protective embrace of my deceased ancestor around me. And, with each crunch of gravel, I summon the troops - "all my relations."

The trail is leafy and peaceful. The rain patters gently over a natural corridor of trees, occasionally opening onto green and gold fields with grazing sheep. The colossal timelessness of my ancestral hills stills me. I come upon a poetry post of my ancestor and read it aloud:

Grant I may so
Thy steps track here below,
That in these masques and
Shadows I may see
Thy sacred way

It feels like a prayer. I decide to let it be one. I walk on while reading, lingering, contemplating the poetry in nature that surrounds us all. There is a bench under an ancient sessile oak inviting me to sit. Swift are the skies in Wales, and I watch the dappled sunlight shimmer on the leaves. A family of mallard ducks drift near the shoreline as kingfishers and kites dart through the trees.

The air here has a scent of destiny. Inhaling, I ponder the secret, interconnectedness of all living things, the presence of spirit, and the existence of a higher power. I think of my serendipitous meeting with Colin and friends and how embracing my ancestral past has made me feel like I belong to my generational family and to the universe.

I read the last poem of my ancestor and I am filled with a sense of peace.

The rising winds,
And falling springs,
Birds, beasts, all things
Adore him in their kinds.
Thus all is hurled
In sacred hymn and order
–Henry Vaughan

Ancestral travel teaches us that there is nowhere to go but forward, and so, like my ancestors before me, I rise in trust and walk on.

Karen Vaughan

COME TO ME

*L*ying in bed one hot, humid morning, I tossed and turned in a half-awake, half-asleep state in my windowless basement bedroom. The night before, I had gathered with friends for a summer backyard barbecue, where we laughed for hours while enjoying delicious food, tropical drinks, and clever jokes. Now, the oscillating fan couldn't effectively cool the space to allow for rest on this fateful Sunday morning around 4 o'clock.

Sensing a surreal presence in my pitch-black room, I amusingly blamed it on the two heavily liquored mojito drinks I drank the previous evening. However, my sensitivities intensified with each moment. Agitated, I slowly turned to my side hoping the sensation would magically disappear. My heart pulsated even faster instead, making me quake from nervousness and squeeze my eyelids tight.

I couldn't shake the fear any longer, and cautiously lifted my head off my sweaty pillow to look in the direction of the "intruder." My eyes nearly popped out of the sockets, as there was an apparition beside my bed, staring at my quavering body. Its form somehow illuminated itself despite the darkness, as though it was composed wholly of light. *Was I hallucinating?* My scientifically trained, logical brain was going bonkers as I laid there frozen, contemplating sanity and reality against what seemed like madness and delusion. No matter which pole I considered wisest, I surrendered to this fantastical presence in my room.

As my sleepy vision cleared, I recognized standing beside me the ethereal form of my great grand uncle, Paramahansa Yogananda. He was known as the father of yoga in the west and was my paternal great grandmother's brother.

I rubbernecked a couple of more times to make sure that my sight was not deceiving me. Rather than wearing the saffron robe he was often depicted in, Yogananda wore a silky white one. His ageless face was more reverent than I remembered, and his "millionaire smile" was more electric than in any picture that I had seen. His countenance was strikingly cherubic and loving, while a brilliant light emanated from everywhere—luminescent, palpable, and undeniable. Yogananda seemed androgynous too, embodying masculine and feminine qualities, so that "handsome" and "beautiful" both applied.

I didn't gain the courage to reach out to touch the untouchable as he quietly surveyed my being with great tenderness. Like a warm blanket, he enveloped me with immeasurable love. My awkward stare stayed cemented on his Divine eyes for what felt like hours. The swami, guru, master, my *Dadu* (Bengali for grandfather) was in my house. Yogananda's gaze turned mischievous and jovial as if this was a regular prank he pulled. Yet the room remained silent.

Yogananda then opened his arms majestic-eagle wide and commanded me with the phrase, *Come to me*, three times. I laid there speechless from the decree. He directed his hands toward me, sending a formidable lightning bolt of electricity into my body. And then, within a few seconds, Yogananda disappeared into thin air, and my humble abode went dark.

As the thunder-stroke of energy coursed through my entire being, my mind entered an enchanted, bewildered state. Every cell, every atom, and even the spaces in between them, appeared afflicted, and my entire body trembled like a high-octane performance sports car. After a while, the Divine electricity streamed gracefully out of my body, leaving a calm nervous system, relaxed muscles, and mellowed mind. The stream of my thoughts softened with each breath while I entered into a state of presence. Deep stillness pervaded my mind, body, and soul, something I had never accomplished before in committed daily practice.

This was a moment of grace where I felt like a baby being held in the Creator's arms, and in a state of Divine coherence, wholeness, and oneness. In Hindu traditions, this powerful transmission is known as *Shaktiput*, which is often offered by mystic spiritual guides, gurus, or priestesses who have attained full enlightenment and genuine mastery. I had been blessed previously with this "descent of grace" by my Divine guru, Mohanananda Brahmachari, as well as the Anandamayi Ma. Yogananda's visit completed a personal Divine Trinity while providing the greatest ancestral gift I could ever ask for.

Little did I know the enormity of the phenomenal moment that had unfolded that June Sunday years ago and overtook my complacent daily routine. For weeks, I played out his auspicious visit repeatedly, marveling at the vision of my *Dadu* in my house and oscillating between cynicism and faith.

The magical visit disrupted a focus on previous roles as a well-paid corporate sales and marketing executive, and on applying myself to mindless, repetitive domestic tasks. My mediocre run-of-the-mill life was gone.

Yogananda had provided a cosmic wake-up call that I couldn't shake off. *Come to me* had become a personal mantra, releasing all unimportant thoughts. I ruminated about my truest purpose regularly, and questioned everything about life–my career, relationships, goals, and values. Gone was the naive notion that the outer form of things really mattered in this world. My definition of success was shifting away from accumulating wealth and material things. At the same time, I felt crazy and sick some days, perhaps experiencing the kundalini syndrome many yogis have complained about.

With my guru traveling around the world, I didn't feel like I could get guidance about or share my experience with anyone in my circle, even family and friends, for fear of being judged. The loneliness of my new Hero's journey became quite evident as I encased and shielded my secret mission in my heart.

Plunging into many spiritual books to search for my answers, I looked for clues in Yogananda's writings and unconsciously fell into old patterns of logic and reason trying to find my sense of authentic direction. Frankincense incense often permeated the air to create deep meditative states as I sat in front of my altar, sometimes for hours. Chanting, mantra, and affirmation repetition, as well as hatha yoga practices were added to my daily practice.

There were many days of major disorientation where I did not want to leave the mysterious realm of my meditative consciousness. Firm answers and spiritual reconciliation were my sincere intent. However, frustration took hold of my heart and derailed plans. Eventually, I simply surrendered in prayer, desperately asking for real guidance, inspiration, and transformation. My strongest desire was to have my *Dadu* come to provide more insight. What did "Come to me" really mean? He did not answer.

Though I seesawed emotionally over a few months, I maintained a devoted spiritual practice of silence. The more I sat in meditation, the more I found myself descending–or ascending—into the depths of my essence, a mysterious realm of unimaginable wonder, beauty, and love. My daily meditation practice became addictive, potent, and spellbinding. My heart opened and I felt a sense of *Bhakti*, or "devotion" in Hindu, to the Universal Spirit (God). I continued to perform my obligations and responsibilities, but now maintained a sense of balance.

With passionate determination and faith, my prayers were finally answered on a beautiful September fall day. A tender and benevolent force wrapped around my being once again. Tears ran down my cheeks as Yogananda, my omniscient, omnipotent, and all-embracing great grand uncle, descended into my consciousness with a capital *C*. The same exquisite smile washed over me. He sat in my third eye and spoke to me from within, sharing instructions for my heroic journey. He cautioned that it wouldn't be a smooth, simple transformation toward my truth, but that he and others would always be present to guide, inspire, and protect me along the way. Yogananda directing me to take the path of self-realization, further reminded me that, in the Spirit of Oneness, all my experiences were gifts not only to inform my evolution, but that of all those whom I touched.

Today, I am honoring my soul on a path toward self-mastery as I serve as a spiritual advisor, bioenergetic healer, and a life architect. Yogananda's presence returns at odd, but regular, times, and is always welcomed. I am still humbled by his tender-hearted, Divine directives, and support, and blessed to be part of his ancestral lineage. *Om Shanti*: peace.

Sujon Datta

AVELINA

*a*velina. It was the name I heard, but of a person I had never met. And yet, for almost two years, I continued to hear the name over and over in my head. When asked, my closest friends and significant other knew no one by that name–alive or departed.

By the time I began hearing Avelina's name, I was four years into my spiritual awakening, and open to receiving signs from Source. As part of this journey of returning to my authentic self, I met a beautiful healer and *manbo* who would help me understand Avelina's ancestral connection.

This healer radiates love and kindness. But make no mistake, she comes with a side of "Don't F@*$ with me," speaking truth whether you want to hear it or not; and for that, I love her.

After hearing me share my struggles and fears about being a single mom, the relationship with my ex-husband and more, she offered the opportunity to partake in a sacred, intimate mushroom ceremony. This experience in the privacy of my home would enable me to connect with my ancestors to receive messages, lessons, and above all, healing. She gifted me a small dose of sacred medicine with instructions, a blessing, and away I went.

The weekend after receiving her gift, my daughters were away for the weekend, so I prepared the space for my journey to meet my ancestors. I showered to cleanse physically, meditated to clear my mental and emotional body, and prayed for clarity and healing while I cleared a space with sage. Then, I took the sacred mushroom and waited.

My journey guide was Pearl, the late mother of my oldest daughter's friend. We had met in 2015 and instantly bonded, as had she and my youngest, who shared a birthday and were called "birthday twins." Pearl had passed away in 2017 from complications of kidney disease, and was here this evening to oversee all that would take place.

As I held space with Pearl, I received visions and messages about Avelina. I was told to stand before a mirror. Doing so was scary because the face looking back at me was one fierce woman. I found myself rubbing my face as if putting on war paint and exhaling with force as if to let out a war cry. My face in the mirror shifted from this ancient warrior to my own. My knees almost buckled from realizing I had met Avelina. That I was Avelina, many lifetimes before.

Once this connection with my ancestral self was understood, I lay down on my bed and learned more. I received confirmation that Avelina led an all-female, indigenous tribe and that I would stop at nothing to protect my ancestral people. Like me, this warrior had two daughters. One was the shaman/healer of the tribe; the other, at age 13, was being prepared to step into a warrior's role. Avelina also had a sister who balanced her fierce and brutal approach to watching over our ancestral people with compassion and love.

Suddenly I saw a man who had the energy of my ex-husband and was shocked to learn that we had known each other long ago. And in that lifetime, as Avelina, I had killed him to protect my tribe–most importantly, my daughters.

Pearl instructed me to lie in a fetal position and allow healing to take place. It felt as if my DNA was being restored, almost as if I was getting power back that I had forgotten existed.

As I lay there, I began to make connections between this lifetime and my previous one as Avelina. My oldest now is a healer who uses a gift for tarot, astrology, and energy work to bring light where many see darkness. One of my closest, dearest friends who came into my life via a broken relationship was Avelina's sister in ancestral times and radiates compassion and love.

Then there's my youngest daughter, who was 12 at the time of my journey. She had been giving herself a year to decide on next steps regarding her homelife, and placed great importance on making this decision when a 13-year-old; I realized now that that would have been when she became a warrior in Avelina's time. And that I too was preparing my youngest for "battle."

Driving the day after my journey, I was behind a public bus with an advertisement on its back for an oat-based drink. "Avelina - A family affair" was the slogan. I laughed at Source confirming what had taken place and affirming that this life is indeed about continuing a focus on family affairs.

In this lifetime, I had removed my ex's life-negating energies rather than killing him physically to protect my family. My tribe as in ancient times: my sister, daughters, and I as their leader. And it is I, Avelina reborn, who will be guiding them into the next phase of their lives.

Lucia Goñez

THE CHRISTMAS ROBE

For my one- to five-year-old children, the Christmas of 1971 was as good as I could make it, given the lack of winter in Hawaii. Listening to carols on the radio and gathering around an imported aromatic pine tree was what my husband Dwain and I could do so our little girls fully enjoyed the Bible story and opening presents.

For me, though, it was a time of mixed joy and heaviness. I had been having trouble sleeping for three nights but blamed it on holiday activities and being due to deliver our fourth child in late January.

I usually am a very heavy sleeper so that, when the children needed me in the night, they would come into our room and awaken me or call out for Dwain. But on these nights, a presence awakened me many times. Thinking it was one of the girls due to the good, loving, comfortable presence in the room, I called out, "Who's there, sweetheart? What do you need?"

Despite Dwain sometimes awakening and noting no one was there, I was certain of the presence, sometimes insisting on checking if the girls were in distress.

When the little ones awakened us on Christmas morning, I was more than a little tired, but set the night visits aside. My mind was filled with the day's tasks for recreating the sounds, smells, and traditions that I had enjoyed as a child with my sister Liz, who was visiting.

The double duty included putting stuffing in the turkey while running back and forth to the living room, checking on what treasures the girls were finding under the tree. After all gifts were opened and tea parties had begun, Dwain insisted I come in for one last beautifully wrapped box still hiding at the very back.

I was dumbfounded when I pulled back the tissue and saw, nestled inside, the most beautiful white satin robe and silk nightgown.

"Obviously you haven't noticed, I'm not the white satin type. I'm going to have four children under five years of age, and we are short of money. I am going to take this back and get a brown corduroy robe that won't show the peanut butter and jelly," I laughingly said.

As I started to put the box aside and lumber to my feet to finish meal preparations, he gently put an arm on either side of my chair and looked into my face.

"You are a white satin and silk woman to me, and you always will be. You are more than just a mother to our children, more than just a cook and cleaning lady, more than just a wife. You are a fascinating, beautiful, and intelligent woman, and we are so fortunate to have you. We love you." He added, "I want you to keep this outfit. Every time you wear it, it will remind you that you are loved very much."

Touching his face, I kissed him, thinking that it was I who was fortunate. Then I put the box on the top shelf of the closet, hoping that, someday, my mother would come from the mainland to babysit, while we went away to rekindle our love.

Any pregnancy can be a burden, a complication in an already complicated life. This one was unplanned and poorly timed, despite practicing birth control. Bethany had just turned one on December 21, and I had been so sick with her pregnancy. Hospitalized twice because of dehydration, I had just barely got my strength back when I became pregnant once again. Dwain was especially distressed over another baby so soon, with the pregnancy stretching our closeness.

However, life frequently "happens to us after we have made our plans." And there is always room for another child at our table. This baby was conceived in love and would be raised in love.

I had known since I was small that my destiny was to have a family and write books. In my mind's eye, a clear picture had always existed of being surrounded by six children. As I went to the kitchen and stuffed the celery and mashed the potatoes that day, I contemplated how unfair life is sometimes-that we were blessed with children in general, while others were not.

My mind kept straying to the "presence" in recent nights. Why had I felt so lightheaded, and why could I suddenly eat a green onion without the pangs of heartburn?

About four o'clock after guests had left, I went into the bedroom to nap. Once again, I felt the comforting presence. But this time, I realized the spirit of my unborn child was no longer in the body I carried in my womb. That was why there was a physical difference in my body and I had felt lighter, almost empty.

I manipulated the womb, trying to get movement, but nothing. Lying on the bed by myself, I prayed that, if what my mind suspected and my heart knew was reality, I be given the strength to carry on. I also wanted our fourth child—and whoever had come through the veil to assist their passage from this world to the next—to know of our love and reverence.

I went to the living room and calmly told Dwain and Liz that I had felt the spirit leave. Liz, a registered nurse, tried to hear a heartbeat, but could only hear amniotic fluid without a stethoscope. She suggested we go to the emergency room.

A nurse, and eventually a doctor, examined me, neither looking me in the eye. I was the calm one. I could tell they didn't want the responsibility of sharing the obvious. Because I had an appointment with my own doctor the next morning, they sent me home.

The next morning, when my doctor asked how I was, I was forthright.

"The spirit left the body of the child I am carrying."

He confirmed this and sat with us for some time, discussing the complexities. He and his wife had lost a child in the same way. He also related stories of mothers who knew when they felt the spirit of a child leave, and others who refused to believe this even with proof.

He asked if I would be strong enough to carry the baby until labor occurred naturally. A caesarean section could have occurred that day, but the fact that the baby I carried was not alive did not bother me. It was still our baby. The spirit had let me know it was alive and would watch over us until birth could occur.

On the morning of January 13th, I went into labor. Dwain and I went to Tripler Hospital, where I had delivered another beautiful baby girl just over a year before. I asked the doctor to anesthetize me so that I wouldn't experience the silence of a birth without a baby's cry.

We insisted on an autopsy in case there was some information that would prove valuable to our other daughters. Our daughter whom we had named Ann Dee was a perfect baby and would have been viable, but the cord was caught around her neck. It was an accident. Nobody or nothing was to blame.

When Dwain arrived that morning, he brought traditional yellow roses, but also the white satin robe. He reminded me of all that we had as a family: each other, our love to sustain us, plus the love of extended family—both here and beyond the veil—who cared deeply about our pain.

We talked about the assurance that Ann Dee Wright was as much a part of our family as our other children, and how we would all be together someday. She later appeared to me in a dream, with light brown hair in a pageboy style. She was tall, wearing a white dress with a rounded neckline and long sleeves. She looked much like her sisters Faith and Bethany appear as adult women. Her sweet smile shown such love at me. I knew then, and I know now beyond any doubt, that her happy spirit lives. She is ours.

I also came to realize that Great Grandma Sarah Elizabeth Turman was the beloved ancestor who watched over us and escorted Ann from this existence into another, more exciting one. Grandma Eula Turman Helm and I talked at length about her mother's sweet spirit. It was right she would have shown such special love and concern for her granddaughter and great granddaughter. After all, in the over 300 direct descendants that came from the union of her and Manford Turman, Ann was the first to leave this world prematurely.

Other gifts that came out of the tragedy of Ann's death included her graveside service and burial. The funeral homes in Hawaii and Utah both refused payment, and Uncle J donated a gravesite that he had purchased for use by the family. Ann's body was buried in Grandma Helm's space. When my mother was later buried, Ann's tiny casket was unearthed and placed above her grandmother's heart. The thought that a great grandmother accompanied Ann in death, and a beloved grandmother will accompany her in the resurrection, brings me great comfort.

Grandparents, I now understand, can recognize the cycles of life and the continuity of family. They are the teachers, not only of traditions and family history, but of lessons of life. That pure love and caring transcends the bonds of earth life and extends for all eternity.

As the years passed and the time was right, we had our Emily, and then Faith, and Andy. My epiphany as a small child has come to pass. And one day, while cleaning out drawers of old clothes, I rediscovered that white silk robe of Ann's Christmas. As I sat on the edge of the bed holding the rag bag in one hand and the robe in the other, my eyes teared while thinking of all the sad and happy times this old robe had witnessed.

It had gotten stained and torn. All the buttons got lost. But I decided to make small pillows from the worn material to serve as a symbol of comfort, love, and hope when someone dealt with menstrual cramps, a broken leg, or the flu. It helped the children feel close to me, even when I was far away.

I made small pillows for each of our children and shared this story. Those pillows have followed them to school, the military, moving all over the world, and having their own children.

We wanted them to understand that they will have the support and love of a departed sister, as well as many grandparents, aunts, and uncles who are beyond the veil of this life. Their ancestors are on their success team. Just as the robe was given as a symbol of deep love to me, I hope they will recognize that they are worthy of this ancestral love and assistance.

Judy Helm Wright

LIFE LESSONS FROM UNCLE GEORGE

I have realized in recent years while recovering from the loss of loved ones including my mother, that none of us knows what tomorrow may bring. So, I was happy to be joining my brother, David, and three sisters on a road trip to see Aunt Martha in Mississippi. That's where my father's people come from, with this aunt among the last two to be able to share memories of our ancestors whom we cherish.

People told me I was crazy to head out from Maryland with four siblings. But David, the executor of our mother's estate, needed to oversee a legal transfer of some property deeds into our names. A close-knit family, we were also eager for some bonding time. Plus, I suspected this journey an answer to prayers about seeing Aunt Martha would be protected by loved ones who had passed.

None of us had more than two hours of sleep before setting out at 4:00 a.m. for the 15-hour drive, yet pillows brought for napping in the car were never used. I think the ancestors knew we had a whirlwind trip ahead and gave us the energy we needed for deep discussions about the state of the world, updates on our nieces and nephews and cousins, and singing along to golden oldies and newer playlists.

When we arrived that evening at Aunt Martha's house in Laurel, Mississippi, we couldn't stop hugging her and our cousin. It had been years since they'd made a 10-day visit to Maryland one Thanksgiving, after gathering a decade earlier at the funeral of Martha's husband, our beloved Uncle George. Nothing beat finally reconnecting in person.

The next three days were a blur of activities planned by our cousin, Karen. They included a walking tour of a neighborhood nicknamed "Bustin Avenue" in recognition of all the houses built there by our grandfather, who was known for his fine craftmanship and honest business dealings. And, at the Laurel Museum, the docent regaled us for an hour with wonderful stories of the residence, the family who'd lived there, and their art and crafts collection. A highlight was a Chihuly glass sculpture, and an amazing collection of Native American woven baskets from each region nationally, presented in the context of the tribes. I marveled at this exhibit, something I'd never seen at the vast Smithsonian in my hometown of Washington, D.C. It seemed the little sleepy town my father was raised in was now all grown up, and I couldn't help feeling proud of what my ancestors and other locals had built.

The kinship connections continued daily, reinforcing my feeling that this trip was coordinated by unseen forces and protective ancestors. At one downtown stop, we sought a family picture in front of a large, muraled wall celebrating the revitalization of Laurel. Finally, a woman came walking by heading to her parked car. One of my sisters rushed over and asked if she'd take a picture of us.

We told her about visiting from Maryland, our dad growing up in Laurel, and being here to visit Aunt Martha. Furrowing her brow, she said she'd known a Martha Bustin, and asked her husband's name. We told her "George Bustin," to which she exclaimed, "Oh my goodness! My husband was George's boss for 40 years at the Masonite plant!"

I bet Uncle George was somewhere in the universe, chuckling at the synchronicities he'd engineered that day, and I silently thanked him for this wonderful surprise.

Gatherings with other cousins and branches of the extended family over the next two days cemented the connection with our Mississippi relatives. On our final day, with the property legalities sorted out, we went back to Aunt Martha's house.

She pulled out several big envelopes full of pictures, shared all the people who were in them, and their family stories. As the evening came to a close, Martha handed us an envelope of pictures to keep. We promised to copy them and to share the stories with our children. Teary eyed, Martha and Karen told us how their whole goal for our visit was to have us learn about our Mississippi family roots, and to walk the land and feel in our bones who our people were.

On the ride back home to Maryland, filled again with energy on two hours of sleep, we recapped the trip highlights that included hearing stories about our dad. He died at age 32, so we had very few personal memories of him. We also heard stories about our grandfather, and Uncle George and Aunt Martha, known as great pranksters. We howled with laughter at some of their former antics, and at the playful teasing between David and cousin Karen.

A retired nurse, Karen had talked about volunteering at a cash-strapped local clinic that provides medical and dental care for the less fortunate. On our way home to Maryland, we decided to make a donation to the clinic to honor cousin Karen and Aunt Martha.

The care needs soon hit closer to home, though, as we learned that Karen's daughter had become very ill with a drug-resistant staph infection from the medical clinic where she works. Her entire face had become swollen, she was hospitalized and being given nutrition and drugs, eventually undergoing surgery that required extensive recovery. We prayed vigorously for her recovery and, in the middle of all this, Aunt Martha had a fall and faced possible hip surgery.

Fortunately, Karen was able to call on former relatives through marriage to help get her granddaughters to and from school each day and to visit Aunt Martha when Karen was visiting her daughter. I call this love and support in difficult times a miracle, and a direct result of Uncle George's life lessons about treating people with love, dignity, and respect.

Two weeks later, when Karen returned to work, it was with a heavy heart. One of her favorite financially strapped patients had called asking if the clinic had any insulin to give away. But when she checked the clinic's refrigerators that day, there was none.

Karen later shared that, when her supervisor asked why she was so drawn to help this particular man, she replied with tears in her eyes that "He has beautiful gray hair, dark-tanned skin, the hands of a laborer, and the same sweet, gentle spirit as Daddy."

But when she'd first met him in 2020, she said he was broken and felt like a failure due to his financial situation. Karen had assured him that wasn't so, and that they'd find a way to get his medications. But this day, she was going to fail him after he had decided to purchase his wife's pain meds and antibiotics instead of his own needed insulin.

At that point, Karen's supervisor simply said, "God is Good" while handing her a card that made her start weeping. It was our donation as the "Northern Bustins" that would permit the man to buy the needed medications.

When Karen emailed later about this, we each had our own good cry. It felt like a full circle moment to learn that we had helped this gentleman reminiscent of beloved Uncle George. Our hearts were full of joy, and our spirits soared. After all, Uncle George was there with us through it all, helping us put into action the lessons he'd taught through his compassionate and steadfast examples in life.

Deborah Ann Bustin

RECONNECTING TO JOY

*H*eart weary and running on empty. Listless, tired, and irritable. A blanket of gray fog has descended, slitting the connection with my inner wisdom. For the last few years, I had worked day and night. My soul connection got lost in the running around, the planning, and the filling in of every minute of the day with finalizing to do's and ticking off checkboxes. When something couldn't be done, I'd lived with ringing in my ears and heart palpitations. I felt deeply miserable but unable to acknowledge that.

Then one spring day, all I had built seemed to deflate, leaving me with empty hands and no clue where to turn. So, I journeyed that night to the land of my soul: a glorious sickle of beach in Spain that allows me to reconnect to the sea—and in this case, to call in a new order for my life. The sea is in my blood from having visited this ancient Mediterranean place for 21 days each year in childhood. This gorgeous land, which for centuries has been guarded by an old castle, is the only place where I was ever able to plant roots.

It is said that wherever land and water meet, fairies and angels are at home. I am equally fascinated by the sea's wisdom and all the treasures, sometimes disguised as debris, beneath her surface. Here in this ancient landscape, I can look to it for inspiration, guidance, and a renewed sense of purpose and belonging.

For one thing, water gives life and takes life. The ocean beckons and repels with its never-ending flow of waves. Ebbing, flowing. This push and pull of water always reminds my soul of the general pulse of things. Her age-old presence urges me to welcome this natural flow graciously into daily life. I'm reminded to prioritize the unfamiliar balancing act of alternating periods of business with periods of rest.

While visiting this beach on my journey, the sea whispers to me of the secret power of the lowest point of the tide cycle, right before the tide changes directions. That this point mirrors my being in a dry spell. I'm made aware that, as much as she needs her dead tides to bring new life into deep waters, I need these moments of feeling "flat, in the middle numbness." They help me to gather my power so that a new space can be opened to dream a more sacred world into being. The waves show me that I need to close one door in order to open another, that a major phase of my life is no longer serving me. I'm reminded that allowing the tide to withdraw permits the something that is beyond my imagination to be welcomed in.

I find guidance, too, in the sea's mutability–that it's important to not take all of life so personally. One day the sea is gray, wild, devouring all. Destroying with glee. The next, beautiful emerald-green waves are dancing elegantly across her surface. I tend to take all that happens in life as being uniquely aimed at me. But life just is. Realizing I can stop owning everything, I sigh deeply as my stomach unknots, and I feel the tension washing away that I had carried so long and hardly noticed anymore.

Beyond the lessons of power, the sea provides essential lessons about renewal. I was buoyed by pondering the transformation of a water drop to vapor, into a cloud, and then to rain to nourish Mother Earth. Water's essence still exists, even while the element's form changes. I have also changed form throughout my lifetimes and beyond yet realize that my ever-present soul is the true me.

The joy this self-acceptance brings makes me long to jump into the waves and dive through them as a dolphin would. When I do, I splash and splatter in the frothy water, ending up feeling as if I am bathing in a huge bath of bubbly champagne fizzing on my skin, rejuvenating me. I stretch out to the sun, seawater droplets leaving tracks of salt on my arms. I acknowledge I need to play more, to let go of the conditioning of continually needing to be productive.

Life is meant to be enjoyed, and I decide to embrace the guidance that stepping into the here and now on this journey has provided. Among the layers of dried seaweed on the shore, some shells have washed up and dried on the rocky, bleached-white beach. Other shells bear the wet of the lapping waves, intensifying their colors, which speak to me. The pearly pink and the bluish gray talk to me about the ever-loving and accepting being of all, God. The soft whistling of the sea breeze, and a seagull's forlorn cry touch me, and underneath it all, the tumble of the surf over the pebbles and golden-colored sand. The message "color" shares with me is that by living my truth, my immense inner strength expressed through open-hearted compassion will become one of my greatest gifts.

More lessons come with taking a beautiful shell in my hand and stroking it. I feel small ridges under my fingertips, and its smooth, pearly inside. Limiting beliefs, I realize, are like the layers of calcium used to build the safe shell that mollusks need. When a growing resident becomes too cramped, the shell would limit growth and thus keep the mollusk small; they eventually must free themselves of their former homes, discarding current limits.

So, it is with the uncomfortable, vulnerable state I am in, needing to shed the old, yet not knowing what is being ushered in. But sometimes there is no choice, for all those layers of limiting beliefs hold you back from allowing in a fresh way of living.

I am glad I trusted my intuition that beckoned me to journey to this healing place to replenish my empty well. With faith, there is a perfect flow for all, as turtles share when they visit my sacred spot every year. Out of the clear Mediterranean Sea they come, climb up the beach and lay their eggs. I ponder their trust of the land to provide protection, safety, and warmth, so their babies will hatch. The hatchlings do so as well when they escape their eggshells and use a deep inner knowing to start their way back into the ocean.

As I walk and the cool, gentle surf laps at my feet, I rely on all my senses to connect with the moment. My eyes take in golden specks whirling up to the water's surface, resembling the way sparkles of energy are being shaken up in me. Helping me to stay in complete wonder and the joy of the now. Gold dust within, fairies waving magic wands to weave rainbows of hope, possibilities, and joy that tingle throughout me.

A sentient, smooth stone held in my hand reinforces the knowledge that all is always transient. The sense of safety we seek from holding fast onto things is a false sense. An illusion. After all, thousands of years of waves broke down a majestic orange-hued rock into smooth pebbles like this one, which contains sparkles of crystals and left-over residue of ancient fossils.

I feel energized too by the heavy, salty, ozone-laden perfume of the air. A deep purifying inhale, and another one. A lightning flash spears at the horizon, emphasizing that new layers of self-care are asked of me. Now.

Never before had I fully realized how much help the ancient landscape offers if I am only willing to allow it. Nature is like a stone sinking in a pond, and thus filling it with beauty and outward ripples. So, it is with my heart as it opens like a flower and I welcome the new balance in me.

A brilliant full moon rises over the sea, painting a silver path on the waters. My intuition and third eye are being activated, raising my consciousness. I am being transported back to my inner, Divine me. The dead tide has been replaced with a renewed sense of direction: to follow the joy. This is all I need to be aware of right now, and to know that the ancestral land and ocean will fill in the how for me.

Florentine Bisschops

THE LITE BRITE BOARD

*B*y the time my brother Dennis left this world in January 2014, we had become friends, and were an important part of each other's lives. We shared talks about politics, life frustrations, and of course, growing up in the same family. This provided the backdrop for healing, both when he was in his physical body and afterward, as I came to understand the larger journey our souls shared.

I wrote a lot about Dennis's traits in his obituary: he was a caring doctor, an involved father, and a witty guy. What he was not, though, was particularly religious or spiritual, with one of his favorite songs being "Losing My Religion" by R.E.M.

His spiritual beliefs did not seem altered as he came closer to leaving this earth. I stayed awake with him on New Year's Eve, 2013, just days before he died. Shortly after midnight, he awoke just long enough to stare into the distance with a perplexed, agitated look and say, "Am I going to have to kick some ass?" I chuckled, thinking that I wasn't sure he'd want to take on whatever it was that he saw.

This felt in line with a brief exchange we had two days earlier when I had said, "You can go whenever you're ready."

"But where am I going?" He asked with a confused look.

His wife assumed Dennis did not recognize that he was in a hospice facility; I took it as a more existential question, that he was unsure of what-if-anything was on the other side.

"Wherever it is you need to go," I answered.

Having personally experienced many connections with people who have passed, especially my husband and parents, I am always curious and excited about what messages they might send from the other side. I wondered if Dennis's lack of spiritual belief would impact his posthumous availability to me.

Although I hadn't heard directly from him at that point, our ancestral connections became clear a few months after his death while meeting with a spiritual counselor and healer. She lived about 45 minutes from Dennis's family, who had come to expect my appointments with Kim whenever I visited them in western North Carolina.

Kim was called to hold our session this beautiful May afternoon outside on a terrace overlooking the mountains. After I shared about my brother's passing and events since, she invited me to lay down and relax on a blanket she had laid out. Soon, the drumming started, and I found myself feeling as though I was leaving my body. My breathing synced up to the beat of the drum. I was still aware of the world around me, yet increasingly connected to the world beyond.

Then the board showed up. It looked like a giant Lite Brite board, a childhood game with pegs that had their colors infused with lights. In the journey, the lights on this spiritual board were being filled in, column by column, with only three colors. To my surprise, I quickly realized that this was an illustration of how my soul, my brother's soul, and my mother's soul had interacted across lifetimes.

In some columns, only two of us were represented, but in most, all three colors occurred. Occasionally a fourth soul would be represented, which I would instantly recognize–be it my husband, father, or a friend. But that soul would only appear for a few lifetimes before the pattern would revert to just me, Dennis, and Mom. Although I could not decipher how the three of us were connected in each incarnation, I was aware our relationships with each other varied widely as we shifted bodies.

In an amazing few minutes, I was offered a high-level insight into thousands of years that I had lived which included Dennis. As the process started to slow down, a voice that seemed to be speaking for all souls that had participated that afternoon offered, *Everything is more perfect than you can possibly imagine.*

Taking several moments and a few deep breaths, I embraced what an honor the experience had been and the profundity of that statement. Gently blinking my eyes open, I returned to take in the beauty of this world and to consider the possibility that everything is more perfect than I could possibly imagine.

Rev. AnnE O'Neil

THE MATCHMAKING OWL

a self-identified mystic, my choices were somewhat limited when seeking a partner, eliminating 90 percent of the men on a dating app I was using. This brought me to Mark, who identified as a mystic and shaman. We started talking and agreed to meet for a dinner date on Monday.

That Sunday, though, I was on a hiking date with another prospective boyfriend, and on our walking trail sat a great horned owl. We backed up to another trail, but after an hour, headed back to the first—only to find the owl exactly where we'd seen it before.

They say that seeing an owl in daylight is an omen from the universe of awakening to wisdom, to learning and seeing the world for what it is, a sign that something or someone is coming to change the very nature of our lives.

I'd had a special relationship with flight and a kinship with winged creatures since I was a little girl. Back then, I had several dreams about flying that had felt so real. And as an adult, I felt the rush of soaring maybe 3,000 feet up when I did a hang-gliding session off the cliffs in San Bernardino. Eye-level with the condors and ospreys was a thrilling experience.

I sensed that the owl needed help and, despite irritating protests from my date that it was dangerous, sought to help it. Having previously rescued a large crow, a robin, and a hummingbird, I knew to approach the injured bird slowly. Kneeling, I asked the owl if it was hurt. It blinked its large yellow eyes once deliberately. I next asked if it would like me to help and received another very deliberate blink. Lastly, I asked if I could pick it up. It blinked again intensely, and I sensed that to mean consent.

Talking to the owl, I told him what I was going to do. Carefully wrapping my soft hoodie around it, it seemed to fall asleep, only occasionally stretching out its leg and uncurling its talons as I carried it about a mile back to my car, where I said goodbye to my date.

At home, my excited teenage children kept our dog away while we began to search for a wild animal rescue center. On an impulse, I also texted Mark. We had planned to have our first meeting on Monday, but I asked if he wanted to come by and do a healing transition ritual for the owl. *He had claimed on the dating app that he was a shaman, hadn't he? It was time to test that.* To my surprise, he said yes, pausing on arriving only to go home to get a drum and rattle.

Despite my kids' anxiety about a man I'd never met before coming to our home, things went smoothly after Mark's arrival. We spontaneously performed a humming and drumming ritual for the owl and gave it some water, which seemed to revive it. We discovered that its beak was bloody and appeared dislocated, suggesting it wouldn't survive long without professional help.

My kids had located a nearby wildlife sanctuary, which provided the first synchronicity for Mark and me. The woman who answered my call asked if I had named the owl; I repeated the question to Mark, and we both replied, "Emma."

The woman excitedly responded, "That's my name too, 'Irma,' which is Spanish for Emma." Mark and I looked at each other in wide-eyed disbelief.

The owl that helped bring us together also helped me see an ancestral guide for the value his religious approach brings to me. My uncle, who had been a Christian bishop in the Syrian Orthodox Church in India, had died a few days before Emma came into my life. I was still grieving his loss, and he had recently appeared to me in a lucid dream. In it, he took off his ceremonial hat and tried to place it on my head, an attempt I rejected. I didn't feel ready to take on any familial spiritual legacy—especially if it meant becoming more orthodox and less hippie mystic.

However, on a date with Mark a few days after our first meeting, he had a spontaneous psychic transmission of my uncle attempting to put his hat on my head again. So, this time I listened.

Meeting that great horned owl has helped me slowly realize that part of my spiritual journey is to honor and own this part of my spiritual legacy. Accepting the value of this ancestor's offering, and being open to having Mark as my boyfriend, are key growth steps I probably would not have arrived at if I hadn't sought to help a new winged friend.

Nina Mathews

REFLECTIONS OF FATHER

My paternal grandmother died in our ancestral home in Kolkata, India when I was 13 years old. At the time, we were gathered as a family in New Delhi, about a thousand miles northwest, to celebrate Durga Puja, a major holiday in India that celebrates the Divine Feminine, when we heard the news.

On the fourth day after her passing, special prayers were to be said in Kolkata for my grandmother. I had a fever early that morning in New Delhi and afterward, I had a vision of my grandmother's serene, happy presence. Alongside her were my grandfather, who had passed nearly 12 years prior, and his equally peaceful sister, who had died many years earlier. My grandmother shared a message for me in our mother tongue, Bengali: that life must not be wasted, and we must treasure the opportunities that come to us as a result of our father's efforts.

This experience remained with me as I became, in my early 40's in the Los Angeles area, a spiritual practitioner of Sukyo Mahikari or True Light. I practice this with my American family and community and with family and fellow practitioners in India. Our practice at home includes serving our ancestors every day in their ancestor altars by offering prayers, flowers, and the essence of food, water, and material earnings.

We all care for our ancestors now and hold ancestor ceremonies for each relative that dies. That included inaugurating tablets for the Banerjee ancestor altar 11 years ago when my father passed away in India. I gave him the astral name Surya, meaning "sun," and wrote it on his ancestor tablet here in my home in Pasadena, California.

My father had been born in a family of landed gentry in Bengal, India. Their family name is an anglicized form of Bandhopadhyay, who descended from one of the sage teachers (Upadhyay) of Bengal. My father's given name, Ashish, means "blessing," as he was and has continued to share spiritual blessings with me. He served in the Indian Army from his youth and rose to the rank of Lieutenant General, serving as the director-general of the National Cadet Corps of India and colonel commandant of the Regiment of the Artillery. For his outstanding peacetime service to India, he received a medal from the president of India.

My father's attitude toward life and conduct was selfless, with few equals. He was widely loved, respected, and trusted while providing an exemplary standard in how he took care of himself, personal belongings, his people, and his country. My mother and he were always punctual too, to not keep anyone waiting. Meticulously fair and honest, he was also deeply loving and artistic.

My last visit to see him in India was in a hospital, where I read a marvelous book on Mother Teresa, and he rested. Nonetheless, we spent several peaceful, heavenly days together in true harmony. When it was time for me to return to the United States, my father stretched out his bony arm and pulled me to his frail and gaunt chest and wept like a child—the first time I had seen him cry.

I sobbed with him, saying, "You have been a very good father to me."

"It has given me immense pleasure to have had you with me," he replied.

Thus, we took leave of each other in an intimate and very personal, yet formal, way. My gifts from my father have included appreciating and cultivating this ability to be present and intimate, yet formal at the same time. During significant moments such as our parting, this capacity of his was especially heightened, allowing us to communicate deeply and with a natural spontaneity and completeness, but with economy. There was nothing extra.

I realize that investing in this capacity, which we all have, helps to communicate deeply, correctly, and gracefully. It assists with developing our discernment and acceptance of Divine will through the ability to remain present and yet non-attached, allowing movement through life with grace and true harmony, whether in daily family and community life or while pursuing the elevation of science, institutions, and civilization. Developing this capacity during my Divine service has assisted my relationship with God and harmony with Divine principles to deepen.

I have also experienced peace and happiness by witnessing the sublime reunion of my father with his ancestors. A few weeks after our farewell, my father's soul passed into the astral realm. My son Rudy was by his side at his cremation ceremony in the greater New Delhi area while I was stuck in California due to travel restrictions. Noticing that there was a spot open for a prayer leader at a monthly Thanksgiving ceremony taking place at the Pasadena Center, I felt compelled to participate.

As I offered prayers as one of the ceremonial prayer leaders the next day, I felt the harmony of my father's warm presence with me. I was extremely grateful to God for allowing us such a Divine arrangement and for granting my father receipt of True Light in his journey in the astral world.

We received signs from nature after his passing as well. I was told that the sparkling morning sky in Noida, India, where my father's body was cremated, turned into pouring rain and thunderstorms. This simultaneously occurred in Pasadena and lasted several days as well, followed by the appearance of a double rainbow in both cities.

Some months later, I awoke from a spiritual dream in which I had seen my father in a boat with his ancestors, gently moving through placid waters in fragrant gardens. A gentle wind emanated from the scene, touching me physically and enveloping me in joy, just as my father's spiritual and physical presence had so often done in this life.

Leena Banerjee Brown, Ph.D.

THE HEALING LIGHT

A flash of light took my grandmother from me; another flash brought her back as a teacher and healer.

Both sides of my family held legacies to be in touch with the sacred, and that was passed on to me. My mother's maiden name in Otomi Toltec was translated to *pájaro* (bird) in Spanish, and she was in communication with birds. The eagle, the owl, and many other birds tell us things about the weather, and they give us omens. My grandmother taught me about special birds that warn us of heavy rain or hailstorms. When I see special birds, I communicate with them by whistles and I'm grateful to understand a little bit of their language. When birds wake up in the morning, they are imprinting the energy in the plants and in the valleys, in the mountains—that's how important their presence is. This legacy from my mother's side is very precious to me.

My grandmother on my father's side received a more mysterious legacy because it was presented through a flash of light we call *centella*—a kind of thunderbolt that sometimes has no sound. And that's a more profound experience. It almost killed her.

My mother was born between Querétaro and Hidalgo in Central Mexico. My father's family lived in an isolated area on the other side of the mountains. They met and fell in love in Mexico City, but when they married, they decided to return to his homeland to live. My mother was immediately accepted by my father's family, in which the men worked as musicians in a band.

My father and his band would play at festivals and parties, sometimes having to carry their instruments to faraway communities. Eventually, they got a big Ford truck. This is a legacy I carry too; I was a musician for the first twenty years of my life, and my son Danzaki now carries on this legacy.

Everyone in my community was a *tule* weaver. All the houses were made of *tule* (bulrushes) and people brought the freshly-cut bulrushes from the wetland and laid it out to dry in the sun. With the men away most of the time, my grandmother was usually in charge of the household. She kept the wives and children of all my uncles doing chores, cutting and weaving bulrush, and making all sorts of meals with the wetland food: ducks, water hens, frogs, fish, shrimps, clams, water beetles, and green plants. My mother wasn't used to this work because she came from another environment, but she did all that she was asked with love and care.

One cloudy afternoon, my grandmother was chopping firewood with an axe out in the backyard. A powerful, soundless light struck her from above and she fainted.

My aunties and my mother ran to her, but she was already gone. She was in coma for two weeks, and then my mother heard her sighing and waking up. My grandmother stood up and asked to be helped to the yard where we used to grow medicinal plants and vegetables.

At the door, she said to my mother, "Please don't come with me, because I'm going to receive something."

So, they let her walk out alone.

Suddenly everyone saw a huge flash of light. My mother and aunties ran outside to check on her, but my grandmother was already walking back, carrying three things: a bouquet of sacred plants, a red leather book, and a huge medallion.

She explained that the great spirit had given these gifts to her. Then she asked my mom to go with her to her room.

My aunties said, "We also want to go."

But Grandma said, "No, because I want to give some instructions to Mila." Mila is my mom.

The other women asked, "How come? She's not your daughter."

"Yes, she's my daughter now and she's the one who is going to receive these indications."

Back in the bedroom, she asked my mother to be sure to put the medallion into her coffin when she died.

My grandmother began to receive instructions in her dreams to heal people, but she refused. At the time, Catholicism was so strong that anybody using traditional medicine was considered a witch. Then she began to feel ill.

My grandmother said to her, "Can you agree with the Great Spirit that you are going to do this healing work just for your family?"

And this is what my mom did. Her way of healing was peculiar; she would put chewing tobacco with saliva wherever it was needed—the stomach, the feet, wherever the pain was—and she could heal any sickness. While she was alive, no member of my family went to visit the doctor. She sometimes used other healing plants, but mostly it was chewing tobacco. She became our family healer.

Remember how I said I started to read and write at four years of age? When I was still very young, my grandfather gave me the red leather book my grandmother had received. It was a little bit heavy for my age, and I was a beginner, but I tried to read it. My grandfather gave me a little stool, and I would sit for a while, reading the book, and then I could go to play with my cousins. I did this every day until I was about thirteen years old.

I didn't understand everything in that book. I sensed what it said, but it's so difficult to remember the words. I know that it talked about caring for life, the connection with all beings, and why we are here as human beings. It said we needed to live in harmony.

So that's the legacy I received. My grandparents had decided I should be the one to read this book. I felt honored, even though I didn't understand it all.

Just before my grandmother passed away, she delivered her healing powers to my mother. I also know how to heal, but my mom is the most powerful healer, because she received those powers from my grandmother.

Grandmother was buried with her medal, and we don't know what happened to the red leather book. It doesn't matter. That wonderful and powerful legacy is still with us, with me, and that's how I am connected to the sacred light of the *centella*, the bright light with a special sound, the sound where mystery is born. This is how our ancestors speak.

Mindahi Bastida

PART THREE

Deepening Your Ancestral Connection

*We are the ancestors of the future and
what we do now will have an impact.*

—LUISAH TEISH

PROTOCOLS AND DISCIPLINE TO DEEPEN CONNECTION

*a*ncestors connect us with our origins. They are everywhere in nature, and this is why nature is so sacred. In order to interact with ancestors in a good and respectful way, we must follow certain protocols or re-create protocols.

In this chapter, we will explore some important protocols: acknowledging original inhabitants of a land, asking permission of major ancestors, honoring clans and what they stand for, honoring the dead, and reciprocity—the protocol of reciprocal taking and giving through offerings and payments. We'll also learn about healing the ancestral lineage. By doing these things, we can help deepen our connection with ancestors. May it be so.

ACKNOWLEDGING ORIGINAL INHABITANTS OF A LAND

To deepen our relationship with ancestors, we need to have an attitude of reverence and acknowledgement of the sacred and the mystery. The attitude needs to come from our individual being, but it is in relation to our collective being, which is in relation to our ancestors. We must have a disciplined practice that always takes time to recognize where we stand in this world and to honor ancestors both in the material and spiritual world.

Every time there is a public or private act of civic or spiritual ceremony, we must acknowledge who was there before us—what species lived there and what peoples inhabited the territory before our existence. Ideally, the acknowledgement will be spoken in the original language and said by a local spiritual keeper of that land. This acknowledgment can also be mentioned at any public gathering by a representative of original peoples and nations or anyone who takes the word in public.

ASKING PERMISSION OF MAJOR ANCESTORS

If you go to a lake, forest, cave, or any other sacred site, you must ask permission to be let in, as these places are major ancestors. This request happens in a ritual format, where you present an offering or a payment to the sacred site as a whole and to the entities and deities that are dwelling in the sacred site. Then you need to listen: Open your heart and your senses and wait for a response. Are you being let in?

When people are not aware of these protocols, or they have forgotten about the important role of the beings, then these beings begin to be manifest in negative ways such as accidents, hurricanes, tornadoes, or earthquakes. At times, a disruption in the harmony of a site happens because of interference with the original configuration or the natural cycles. Ecologists and conservationists speak up and try to help, but the reparation needs to be sealed by spiritual authorities, because they know how to communicate with the entities and deities.

Much of what we have seen happen in the last generations is because our relationship with our ancestors is broken. We have not taken into consideration that they are always there to guide us, and when they have communicated to us in regard to the way that we need to live with Mother Earth, we have failed to follow their directions.

HONORING CLANS AND WHAT THEY REPRESENT

In many communities and societies when there are festivities or rituals, ancestors are invoked by clans. We must respect this ceremonial act and those who perform it; if we are initiated into a clan or a sacred practice, we must be disciplined about it. To honor the spirit of thunders, clouds, volcanos, and more, people from each lineage reproduce specific dances and music, and wear ceremonial attire. The Bear clan people carry out their dances to honor their ancestral lineage and so do the Deer clan, or Snake clan, or Eagle clan. When they dress as the animals they are connected with and perform the dances, they can share that connection with others, and this increases our level of sensitivity about caring for sacred places and their inhabitants.

Clans also carry out special rituals through pilgrimages to sacred sites. Some of these sites have one or two sacred elements—the fire, the wind, the earth, or the water—that are prominent. Certain *mamos* from Sierra Nevada de Santa Marta, Colombia, work with the waters. They work to ask the waters to come back again after they have gone. Mothers of the waters carry out ceremonies for all the waters, including hidden spring waters. They see waters even in the sky. Other spiritual leaders and the families are related to volcanos, and they perform ceremonies for the spirit of volcanos, which are very beautiful.

The level of complexity in relationships can go even further. There are some spiritual leaders that are in relationship with certain celestial bodies such as the Sun, the Moon, and even more distant planets and certain stars in the sky. They are the clans of those celestial bodies.

HONORING THE DEAD, *DÍA DE MUERTOS*

Since ancient times, Mexico has honored its ancestors in a major celebration that takes place every year in the month of November. In the highlands of Mexico, where the Otomi-Toltec tradition prevails, forty days before, in September, utensils and drinks are prepared and the *cempaxúchitl* flower is planted so it will be ready for the offerings. In most houses, the offering is prepared at the altar, which becomes filled with decorations of *papel picado* of bright colors such as Mexican pink, purple, blue, green, orange, and yellow. Flowers, candles, and food fill the space in a beautiful array.

The colors, flavors, and aromas that make up the offering are varied, according to the region. The offering is decorated with flowers. In some places, bows are prepared. Living spring water, or holy water, is an important feature. Candles also are part of the offering; each one represents the soul of an ancestor.

The first souls that are expected to arrive are the souls of ancestors who died by accident, on October 29th. On the 30th, those who died and did not receive a name are received. On the 1st, children and those who died without getting married are received. On November 2nd, older people or adults are received. In the first days, the most basic of the offering is placed: flowers, candles, water, fruit, and a little food. To receive the children, *tejocotes*, sweet potatoes, *chayotes*, oranges, peanuts, and sweets are placed. Sweet tamales and atole and hot chocolate drink are prepared for them, among other traditional drinks. Over the night of November 1st and into the dawn of November 2nd, the offering is completed with fruit. Turkey or chicken mole is prepared and drinks such as mezcal, tequila, or pulque are placed at the altar. Candles are also added to welcome adults.

At dawn on November 1st, a path of white flower petals is placed from the sidewalk to the altar. Prayers are made with an incense *copal* to prepare for the coming of the ancestors, and the door facing east is left ajar. Then at dawn on the 2nd, yellow flower petals are placed on top of the white ones.

In some localities, breads of the dead with pumpkin seeds are placed at the altar, too, as well as the fruits that people liked during their lifetime, such as orange, guava, and boiled *camotes*.

It is important to mention that the passing of the dead is not to be lamented at this time; the holiday is a ceremony to celebrate our connection with our ancestors, acknowledging that they have transcended. People are happy because they are going to receive their ancestors, and a deep connection is cultivated with them in that level.

Some people go to the cemetery during the day to light candles and leave flowers. In other places, the ritual of lighting candles and placing flower petals around the grave takes place at night. The relatives of the people who have left, both adults and children, visit each grave, and the cemeteries become filled with candles. It is a spectacular view surrounded by the aromas of the *cempaxúchitl* flowers. This memorable experience is a chance to be with the ancestors who have transcended. During the vigil, the elderly take care to keep the candles with dignity, upright.

At dawn on November 3rd, everyone returns home and the offerings at the altar are gathered. Elders say that fruits, breads, and drinks have already lost their aroma and their essence, but that they have to be shared, so baskets are filled with mole, tamales, breads, and fruits and shared with nearby neighbors and *compadres*. Some food is brought to the home fireplace or kitchen to heat it up on the *comal* (hot clay pan) or in clay pots. Everybody gathers at the dining table to share and complete the celebration.

There is a tradition in which children ask for "their little skull." They go from house to house asking for a piece of fruit or a coin to be able to enjoy these festivities. The Day of the Dead is a celebration of ancestors, but also celebrates the continuity of life. The ancestors return to where they had lived and have an opportunity to contact their relatives. How beautiful it is to live those mystical moments of joy, where relatives gather in communion with their beloved ancestors.

RECIPROCITY: OFFERINGS

Interacting with ancestors requires us to understand and practice the principle of reciprocity. For this, it is necessary to distinguish between offerings and payments, for they entail different levels of commitment, experience, and responsibility.

Offerings are presented in ceremonial acts to make a request or to give thanks for a favor received from the ancestors. Elements in offerings generally consist of flowers, fruits, tamales, sage, or *copal* (sweet pine resin), tobacco, water, clean soil, stones, seeds, and artisan alcohol. Unlike payments, which require a personal effort to produce, offerings can be purchased at local markets.

When presenting an offering yourself or participating in one led by someone else, keep your mind focused on good, pleasant, clean thoughts so the offering is received by the entities and spirits in a good way. When setting up the offering, be sure there are lit candles, ideally in the four directions, so that the fire is present. Also light incense and include flowers so that beautiful scents fill the air. Bring in the other two elements, water and soil, represented by stones and seeds.

Start by acknowledging the major ancestors in the four directions where there are sacred sites and bioregions. Name all the beings that you can remember that live in the place where you are. Include animals, plants, and people. Recall your maternal and paternal ancestors as well. Then clearly state why you are presenting the offering. This is important because words imprint on the offering the energy that ancestors will receive.

You might be expressing gratitude for something granted to your community or yourself; or you might be asking ancestors for guidance or to open doors and paths that will make your life better or facilitate the healing of your community. This act, when done with a humble and open heart, strengthens the spiritual interconnection between ancestors and the person, their family, and their community.

Offerings can vary in format, size, and content. A group offering can be done with family members or loved ones who are close to you, or it can be done with the whole community. Some offerings are monumental and require hundreds or thousands of people; in these cases, special people spend weeks collecting everything that will be needed. The offerings will include flowers, fruits, seeds, paper, woven bulrush, or woven palm. The air will be filled with incense and *copal* (sweet pine resin), as well as the sounds of ancient and modern instruments. At the opening and closing of these events, a discourse is offered by the spiritual authority.

RECIPROCITY: PAYMENTS

Spiritual payments are important and require greater responsibility than offerings. They are more elaborate and there is more time and effort involved in obtaining all that is needed for the delivery at the ceremony.

Payments are made as an act of reciprocity for what we have spent or for what we have taken in our lives. You pay, for example, for all the oxygen that has been breathed, for all the food that has been consumed, for all the water that has been drunk, for the energy of the Sun that we have received, for the breezes of air received, for everything that the eyes have seen. We pay for the paper that we have used and for the metals that make the technology we use. We pay for the coal that brings electricity to our homes and the copper in the wires. We pay for the plastic and all the products that come from oil. We pay for all that communities in biodiverse regions suffer because of mining, logging, and oil drilling.

We pay Mother Earth for everything that is given to us without us giving anything in return. In this act, participants humbly recognize that nothing we experience or have can be taken for granted.

A payment must be prepared over days or several months or moons, and it may take a year or more to gather everything that is going to be needed. Generally, flowers and fruits are cultivated, candles and incense are prepared, stones and crystals are collected, pure water is collected from various places, clay or vegetable fiber figures are made, honey is harvested, feathers and beetles are collected from the forest, and secretions from the body are collected. Each of the elements is treated with care and kept in a safe place on the altar. There they are frequently blessed by household members.

As the day approaches, special food and drinks are prepared. On the day of the ceremony, the place where the payment will be presented is cleaned, first with a special broom, then with flower water, then with sweet-smelling incense. To do this, the traditional priest first speaks with the entities of the place, which ideally is a place in nature that is considered sacred or special. The spiritual authority explains to the entities that people want to present an offering and asks their permission. A woven mat or an embroidered blanket is placed on the clean surface and all the elements are arranged in the most beautiful display possible. The ancestors greatly appreciate aesthetics, and this beauty we co-create helps our psyche to raise the connection with the Great Spirit, the ancestors, and the entities. All or part of the process can be accompanied with harmonious music or songs.

When the ceremony is about to begin, the roads to the four directions and to the heart of Heaven and Earth are opened with a fanfare of sounds from ceremonial instruments. The person in charge of the ceremony invokes the ancestors and presents them with each of the elements of the payment. In many cultures, everything that is presented is named in diminutive as a gesture of respectful reverence, such as "We bring you these little flowers, this little fruit." Everything is done and said with love, softness, and respect so that the payment will be well-received.

Once the ceremony—which may include a vigil—is complete, part of what is presented is buried or deposited at the foot of trees or hung on branches, or left beside a nearby spring or stream, or at the entrance of a cave. Some things, like feathers and flowers, are distributed among the participants so that they can take it back to their own altars and continue to maintain the connection with the ancestors in that way.

With this act, we ensure that harmony, health, and good life will be maintained for everything around us—which is the collective family—and beyond, because the ancestors communicate with each other, and if one is happy, the others resonate with that good energy and keep everything in harmony.

HEALING THE ANCESTRAL LINEAGE

Many of the lineages in the world have been partially or fully lost, and with it has gone the practice of responsible reconnection with nature, Mother Earth, and celestial bodies. In a few cultures, this practice that started hundreds or thousands of years ago continues today. A distorted perception led people to lose the sense of reverence for what creates and nurtures life. Instead of co-participating in the processes of nature, many started to try to control and exert dominion over nature, as well as dominion over people and territories. The laws of nature were put aside so these people could impose the so-called "Divine laws" and man-made laws. The laws were meant to subjugate and manipulate others and ultimately to accumulate wealth—even if that meant breaching states of natural balance in ways that might have long-term repercussions.

In this man-made regime, laws about protecting nature are permissive, for they are always in tandem with profitable development plans. Under the dominion framework, every place in the world is vulnerable: even pristine places, or places that local people have kept almost intact, are susceptible to exploitation of the waters, land, and people.

The unfolding of complex financial, military, and religious institutions and structures, with long-term plans, is happening before our eyes. One of the oldest institutional plans that has enabled this dominion process is the 14th century Doctrine of Discovery through the Papal Bulls (pronouncements from the Catholic Church). The Doctrine of Discovery stated that European explorers, whom the Church considered biologically "superior" to native people, had the right to conquer any land or people they discovered. The effects of this idea are still being felt today in many countries around the world.

Knowing how interconnected we are, it is probable that in your own lineage, or the lineages of the people in your circle of interactions, includes a traceable history of impacts made to waters, land, and people. This damage can be healed if you begin working on it with an open heart and with responsibility.

EXPLORING OUR ANCESTRAL LOCATIONS

Some people research their genealogy as a hobby, at a superficial level. But a nicely printed family tree is only the first step to exploring about your foremothers and fathers. What comes next runs the risk of finding information that can turn out to be highly significant. To undertake this task, we must be ready to find out what things people in our lineage did that had repercussions on their descendants and in the extended community.

The first step is researching about the history of the place where our ancestors lived. How was that family linked to a particular territory? Of course, both the father and the mother history lines are important, as they complement each other. Perhaps the father lineage or mother lineage has been there for generations, and has even had the opportunity to grow roots, thus perhaps contributing to the resilience of the place. If you did not partake in that process (having grown up elsewhere), try to go to the place and (re) connect.

Some families experienced migrations or exiles. You should find out what caused family or personal displacement. If it was by force, the rupture and pain has probably not been healed. In this case, it is advisable to go to the place of your ancestors and reconnect. If possible, you could consider returning to live there, to pick up the thread of the family and work on healing. But even visiting and making an offering can help release trauma contained in the family DNA.

When looking into how an ancestor arrived at a new place, be ready to ask whether there were native peoples there at the time, or native people who had already been driven out of that area. A caring ancestor would have dedicated time to honor the territory and the people who inhabited it in multiple ways. If you believe that such connection did not happen, then do it yourself. In acknowledging the place and the people and showing loving respect and reverence, a sense of communion unfolds—not just within you, but throughout your lineage to the past and the future. This kind of healing is so needed in the world.

THE LEGACY OF OUR LINEAGE

For each of the ancestors that most resonate with us, we can learn about how they lived and what they did for a living. It is good to find out about their skills and jobs, as often the jobs are related to the place itself. Also, skills are generally passed on, either by instruction or genetic heritage. Our wise elders say that inherited talents represent responsibilities which must be preserved, cultivated, and honored.

If ancestors were musicians, dancers, writers, painters, spokespersons, religious workers, fishermen, beekeepers, woodcarvers, stoneworkers, or smiths, one can easily recover the knowledge and be in service to the community in that way. Additionally, there may be seeds, tools, recipes, books, music pieces, designs, or buildings that some of your ancestors left, and those can become significant to you or the community.

It might also be necessary to make a thorough revision of the value system, belief system, and cosmovision instilled by the community and family, particularly by the religious authority or head of the family—who may have been a woman or a man, depending on the tradition and the circumstances. Many times, in spite of (or because of) the religious faith, our relatives maintained practices that were vicious and destructive. They might have made profit from selling and exporting ancient artifacts, precious stones, ceremonial objects, or even pieces of buildings. This kind of attitude perpetuates the karma of a lineage.

Sometimes, the skills in a family lineage have been used in immoral or destructive ways. Here, too, we need to take responsibility to clean the karma. This is true of the families of miners, oil diggers, and water engineers who have helped destroy the landscape and ecosystems. It is also true of those who make profit from selling and exporting oil, minerals, precious stones, waters, wood, seeds, nuts, fibers, animal furs, ivory and organs, medicinal plants and fungi, spices, fruits, fish, and farm products. It is also the case for those who used slave labor to extract at the highest speed possible, with the least financial investment.

ADDRESSING THE WRONGDOINGS

When you feel spiritually prepared or are instructed to—and if you want to resume responsibilities in your lineage, your clan, or your people—it's advisable to address the acts of key members of the family, and as much as it may be hurtful, unpack that. You may need to go to the place where the damage was perpetrated and perform a ceremony to release that suffering. Ideally, do this with your close relatives or people who love you and respect your process. If necessary, take a special ceremonial person who is trained for this kind of task.

Prepare bundles to offer, and in the process, especially consider returning land, relics, sacred objects, "war trophies," and even dignifying posts in office at specific decision-making spaces. It takes a conscious member of the family to assume the mission of giving back. It is a difficult undertaking. You will have to consider that, aside from repatriation, there must be complementary retribution—one that is proportional to the number of generations that could not carry out their traditional practices because of the fragmentation of their ceremonial system.

Some people take a DNA test to try to understand more about their lineage. When you do this, be ready to take on the responsibility that comes with this new information. One very beautiful realization is that we as humans are so much more related than we think in terms of major ethnic groups and biocultural territories. This can bring a sense of brotherhood and sisterhood that is very healing.

Also, some people dream of an ancestor and opt to explore all about their life, their purpose, mission, accomplishments, and pending tasks. This kind of disciplined work is recommended. It will surely help you understand why your life has unfolded as it has up to this point, and what might await you if you address apparently irrelevant issues from people in your genealogy.

IN SACRED CONNECTION

*W*e are not alone, and we have never been alone. Our ancestors are speaking to us, watching us, and guiding us. When you go to a place where you really feel that connection, you need to follow your feelings and let that connection unfold. You can then receive what is meant to be received by your body, your soul, and your spirit.

Whenever you have a problem, you can consult with your ancestors; you can pray and ask them for help if you remember and invoke them. That's the beauty of the past and the present. Our ancestors are the reflection of how we are living in this world, but in sacred connection, in a sacred way of being. This can only happen when we are conscious of existing in a collective way.

We experience connection through energy. It is important how we develop our minds, our rational ways of thinking. We must learn to conduct our thoughts in a beautiful way so that we can live in positive relationship with all beings. We have a responsibility to avoid damage, exploitation, or disturbance of any kind. On the contrary, everything we do in our minds, with our words, with our hands, or with our energy must be to encourage the flourishing connection with the beings and entities that are dwelling there.

To live in this way is to live with an open heart, showing others how to live while reveling in the beauty of this world. This practice was inherited from the origins, and it may or may not have been inherited in your family. But you can cultivate it and inculcate it in your progeny and make it part of whatever you carry out. The beauty that you care for is reflected in your being and in what you do.

In this chapter, I would like to offer reflections about living in reverence with Mother Earth; the ceremonies that can help you; and guidance for the continued work of connecting with ancestors.

LIVING WITH REVERENCE FOR MOTHER EARTH

Since ancient times, indigenous peoples and nations have lived in reverence of Mother Earth. This is how a sacred interrelation with life is generated.

Life is possible when the four sacred elements are present: fire, air, water, and earth. Caring for life begins with acknowledging and honoring the sacred elements and the way they participate in the emergence of life. All beings hold the four sacred elements. Plants and animals grow and create complex communities when there is a healthy, balanced state of the four elements in the environment.

For human beings and other creatures, life is held by sound energy, light energy, and plasma energy, which interconnects the material, mental, and spiritual dimensions. Matter, thoughts, and spirit unite in trilogy through energy; many creatures are conscious of this. That is why whales fill up the ocean with sound vibrations and birds fill the forest with songs. In savannahs and grasslands, crickets bring everything to the same frequency of sound energy: the rocks, the waters, and the hot air all become one. To commune with nature in this way, in these special moments, is an act of reverence.

The purpose and meaning of life is to acknowledge the interconnection and transcendence of all beings, including Mother Earth. As human beings, our presence on Earth is for the care of life, which can flourish only when it is balanced and healthy.

The original peoples and nations have lived in a harmonious relationship of reciprocity, respect, and responsibility for the territories and ecosystems where they live and beyond. From them, we can learn to live in harmony with nature and with all expressions of life.

Where there is greater cultural diversity, there is also greater biological diversity; the biocultural diversity is the biocultural heritage. This is because your way of thinking, acting, and feeling is based on a philosophy of respect for life. That respect becomes a responsibility, and it is reflected in the way you choose to live. You live with the land and not from the land, and you keep a discipline in relation to the ones who enable us to live. You are always thinking about how to reciprocate and taking the necessary steps to do so.

Today, 80 percent of the biological diversity in the world is in the territories of the original peoples and nations. This is because the original peoples and nations of the world live in co-responsibility. These peoples, who represent barely five percent of the world population, care for more than half of the world's territories. They also care for what is intangible like sacred songs, music, ceremonies, which is part of caring for all of Mother Earth. But because we are in a crisis of civilization, and an overwhelming globalization, the territories of these peoples are under constant threat. The civilization crisis and climate crisis also affect local peoples and communities.

The wisdom and knowledge of ancestral cultures is valuable if it helps us recognize and reconnect—through intercultural dialogue and collective efforts—to regenerate our interconnection with life. Living in reverence with Mother Earth means reconnecting with our origins and ancestral principles.

Today, native peoples and nations; local and international organizations; national governments and international institutions must unite to face this global systemic crisis that threatens not only the individual and the community but also the complex system of life. The biocultural erosion is becoming stronger. It will only be possible to reverse the destruction collectively.

Humanity is experiencing the end result of a dogma that dictates domination of life. To change the history of destruction, fragmentation, and disharmony with nature and ancestral peoples, it is important to return to the sacred original principles and consider the ancestral wisdom and values. The whole of the human family must realign to these values, to ensure the recovery of harmonious life systems. Everyone, but especially original peoples, play an important role in buffering the impacts of climate change events and in preparing wisely for the coming impacts to our coasts, lands, and bioregions.

These strategies may not come fast enough for life to unfold in harmony for the coming generations. Urgent measures must be taken to ensure simple things: clean and healthy water bodies; harmonious weather; clean and healthy air and soil; clean energy; plentiful seeds and food systems; and harmonious biocultural regions with thriving communities. All this will enable us to live well, in harmony, responsibility, and respect for life.

To revere life is to revere the ancestors. It means taking care of life and taking care of ourselves and the generations to come. Only in this way can we complete our transcendence as humanity and as an all-encompassing family of species and beings.

That is why we need to be interconnected with the Divine creation. We must think positively in a clean way, with clean thoughts. Let us not think *about* Mother Earth, but think *with* Mother Earth and all her beings. This is an opportunity to recover dignity, peace, and the flourishing of the human species in relation to the web of life.

WATER CEREMONY

One of the most important water ceremonies consists of inviting a girl or a boy, with their mother's consent, to present flowers to living waters—a river, spring, lake, or some other water body. The ritual begins with a greeting to the four directions. Then the traditional priest sings a song with a drum or other instrument. The priest refers to the water as a sacred element and calls for the hidden waters, springs, clouds, rivers, creeks, and all water bodies.

The traditional priest asks an elder to share a message or a song. Then the priest blesses all people attending with water; if possible, by putting some drops from a flower (dipped in a bowl of water) into the hands and on the forehead of every person present. Otherwise, the priest sprinkles drops of water on the people, sky, and earth with a flower.

Then the child presents flowers to the living water, while saying: "Here we are giving respect, giving these precious flowers to you. Thanks for your love to us, thanks for feeding all beings. You are sacred and we love you."

If the people who accompany have flowers or prayers to offer, this is the time to do it. The ceremony comes to a closing with this act.

CEREMONY OF THE FOUR DIRECTIONS AND FOUR ELEMENTS

One of the most important and transcendental practices to reconnect and deepen the relationships with the ancestors is through the ceremony of directions. There are many ways to carry out this ceremony. Here is the easiest way to do it.

First, you collect elements for the offering and make an altar; your altar can be simple, but it is important to set one up. If you will make the ceremony with more people, invite them to participate in its preparation. The offerings should represent the four sacred elements: fire, air, water, and earth, in this order, which in my tradition are related to the east, the north, the west, and the south, and to the sunrise, the sky, the sunset, the ground, and the underworld beneath. For the fire, candles are placed; for the air, feathers and sound instruments are placed; for the water, water gourds are placed; and for the earth there may be flowers, fruits, seeds, or crystals. Everything is cleansed with incense or sweet grass or *copal* (sweet pine resin).

Once the altar has been made, the first direction to which the prayer is directed is the east, where the Sun rises. If there are more people, make a circle; if it is few people, spread out evenly, having the four directions as the main markers. Prayers are started with the sound of a conch shell blowing three times.

All the entities that live in the direction of the east are recognized, including sacred sites, the peoples, the traditions, and the deities. In the case of Mesoamerica, the presence of the feathered serpent is recognized as a deity that comes to reactivate each era.

Then one goes to the west. With three sounds of the conch shell or some other instrument, the prayer is directed to the place where the veil of the night covers everything in mystery. The feminine place of birth and of death is recognized, along with all peoples, cultures, traditions, and everything that lives in that direction. We request strength to continue the path of light and offer gratitude to the universe for being present in this life.

Immediately, one turns to the north, the place of white snows. Three blows of the conch shell or three sounds of another instrument open the prayer space. Prayer starts by recognizing everything that exists in that direction and remembering the times of the last ice age. Sacred animals and plants are recognized as well as the teachings that emerged from the sacred sites of the temperate forests of the north and the lakes and plains and great canyons. Everything that exists in the north is acknowledged.

Then, over the right shoulder, one looks south, represented by the yellow color of the earth, flowers, honey, and fruits. With three musical notes, the prayer opens to recognize all entities and all peoples who live in that direction. Likewise, the cultures that have emerged since time immemorial are acknowledged. Temperate forests, deserts, sacred plants and animals, and all sacred sites in that direction are honored.

Giving a complete turn to the right, we look towards the center and up, sending three musical tones from our hearts to the heart of the sky, raising our arms. The Great Spirit is thanked for life. The old father and mother are recognized for being aware of our presence in this world. The universe is recognized, and the heart of heaven, too. All spirits, entities, and deities are asked to continue to protect us and bless us in this walk of life.

Then one touches the ground, bending the knees, and with three more musical notes, one prays to Mother Earth. We apologize for all the damage that has been done to our Mother, and we thank her for all the fruits and the beauty that she offers us, day by day. We also thank Earth for everything she has unconditionally provided in the past, including all that our ancestors received and what future generations will receive. We remember here that we are traveling in the universe with our Mother and that our Mother has her relatives, her ties with other celestial beings, and that we are here as her children. We are grateful for everything she gives us.

At the end of the ceremony of the directions, a complete turn is made, so that one looks to the center of the circle. Bringing the hands to the heart, we say thanks for the presence of all who are participating in the ceremony, and each one is blessed with three sounds of the conch shell or other instrument. We give thanks for the opportunity to carry out this ceremony and for the strengthening of the relationship with the ancestors from the past, in the present, and in the future life.

CONNECTING TO THE QUARTER MOMENTS OF THE DAY CYCLE

The most important practice to connect with the heavenly bodies that we call ancestors is by following the Sun at sunrise, noon, and sunset.

Grandparents told us that only the lazy do not see the sunrise. They told us to honor the sunrise every day. So one begins by looking to the first rays of the Sun. Remove your hat. The Sun's rays are a blessing from Father Sun and they combine with the rays from the stars in the region at that time of the year. This energy gives us the strength to begin the day and our daily activities.

One can extend the hands as a sign of receiving that energy and close the eyes without thinking about anything. Some say a prayer, recognizing the mystery of the new day as an opportunity to remember who we are. Birds and many animals greet the Sun at this time, helping us to understand that we are connected between heaven and earth.

Your sunrise ceremony can last from three to fifteen minutes. It is important to recognize the ancestors in the landscape. Observe the terrain, the valleys, the waters, the peaks of the mountains, because that is how we recognize where the Sun comes from and its relationship with the landscape.

The second opportunity to connect with the Sun is at noon, when the Sun is at the zenith. People who are in the field, in the water fishing, or at work can suspend their activity for a few moments to reconnect. It can be done in silence or with a prayer, depending on the religious practice of the person. The zenith is a moment when the Sun radiates toward all beings, and we can feel that connection with the sacred, recognizing that the Sun gives life energy to everything in the ecosystems, starting with plants and algae.

The next time to connect with the Sun is at sunset, just as the light is disappearing under the horizon. This moment is important because it is when the stars begin to appear and when the birds are saying goodbye. We feel the breeze blow and, if we are lucky, we might see the twinkling white-blue light of Venus. We connect with the mystery of this time of transition into the night when the sky will cover us with its starry mantle. We can extend our hands to bid farewell to Father Sun, who has given his energy one more day.

Three important times to meditate are at three in the afternoon, at midnight, and at three in the morning. These moments are crucial, as they help us recognize that we are one more species in the concert of life. If we can synchronize with the animals that manifest in these times, we can observe their disposition and dedication to that very sacred moment. This helps us learn to reconnect with the mystery of life.

We must also connect with the Moon—both the New Moon, when the Moon is close to the Sun, and the Full Moon, when it is opposite the Sun. These moments are important. We must pay close attention to the days in the monthly cycle, so we can receive guidance from Grandmother Moon.

This practice was carried out by our elders. I always saw my grandfather pausing and taking off his hat on the three special moments of the day. Both he and my father instilled in me the importance of this ceremony. It is an offering to all beings on the Earth and to the heavenly bodies that help us live fully. When we put all our intention and disposition into such moments of synchrony, it generates a three-dimensional energy that is both restorative and harmonizing.

GUIDELINES FOR FURTHER WORK TO CONNECT WITH ANCESTORS

- **Continue the work of light** to stay at the level of conscious awakening.
- **Get together with like-minded people**, with the same ideas, values, and spiritual practices, to do ceremonies and make pilgrimages.

- **Approach spiritual leaders of original peoples** to learn about their philosophy and check within to see and feel what resonates with you.
- **Attend ceremonies that honor ancestors**, especially when they resonate with your lineage and when they are celebrated in your territory.
- **Participate in collective efforts to heal nature and restore her balance and harmony**. There is great satisfaction in seeing how you have helped nature recover and look beautiful again.

REFLECTIONS TO BE IN TUNE WITH ANCESTORS

We need to take care of our body, our thoughts, and the spirit when we are in conscious interconnection with other beings. How does my mind process the experience of interrelation with another person, a plant, or an animal?

As human beings we need to take care about what we eat, drink, and consume in general. How much did I interact with what I am about to eat, drink, use, or wear?

We need to observe our ego and quiet it down, so that authentic good feelings can flourish. How is my ego reacting to what is said about me, my family, my community, my ancestral lineage, and my territory? How can I build up the dignity of my community without letting the egos of leaders get in the way?

To accomplish transcendence, we need to be interconnected with the Divine creation. How do I practice spirituality and cultivate connection with the Divine?

To feel in connection with Mother Earth and all her beings, I must connect with my heart, letting beautiful thoughts flow by. Most importantly, I must not think *about* Mother Earth but *with* Mother Earth and all her forms of life.

May reconnection with our ancestors heal us as much as it heals them and our descendants. We must not forget that we are here just for a while. Let us show appreciation to be alive and well in every act. As we go about our lives, let us openly love Mother Earth.

Making the declaration "I love Mother Earth" is especially powerful. Make a commitment to declare this at least once a day.

FINAL THOUGHTS AND BLESSINGS

O ur ancestors are the reason we are here in this world. They have helped us polish both our personal and our collective identities, which gives us the reason to live. Our identity is based on the original principles of reciprocity, reverence, respect, love and, above all, responsibility to care for life. These principles give us an orientation to good living.

Contact with our ancestors strengthens our identity because they are the origin, the root of where we come from; if we know where we come from, we know who we are. Then we know how we can be of service to those who come in future generations. We will have the elements of identity to lead them. The future is in the past and the past is in the future in this three-dimensional interrelation that is generated in the present moment.

Identity is essential to interconnect us, both tangibly and intangibly, with the mystery of life. The inheritance of our ancestors helps us stand in the world in such a way that we know who we are—if we recognize the root of where we come from. Because we are the hills, we are the mountains, we are the river, we are the caves, we are the lagoons, we are the sea, we are the sky, we are the stars, we are the valley, we are the air, and we are the sacred elements, and even fossilized life.

In fact, we are the legacy of our ancestors and we will be ancestors in the future, so the legacy must always remain in connection with the sacred origin of life. That is why we must understand that our legacy is a deep responsibility. We come to this world with a task. That is why we must take care of the principles and values of our ancestors. Likewise, we need to take care of ancestral elements and everything that gives us identity, such as language, dances, traditions, customs, and spiritual practices that connect us with other species and other entities, deities, and the mystery of life.

Our identity is the collective heritage that our ancestors have inherited from their ancestors. It is transmitted from generation to generation. We want to deliver it in a good way to those who are to come to this world.

The ancestors include people that we have loved, those that we continue to love, and those who are living to be loved in the future. Among the ancestors we find family lineages, the extended family, and the diverse community. We also find the clans with whom we are related.

In larger community there are also beings, entities, and the deities to whom we relate. There are beings of the waters, like the mermaids, the beings of the sky, like the lightning and the spark or the feathered serpent. There are beings that have a presence in this world and in other dimensions. We recognize the beings of the caves and the entities and deities that inhabit or take care of the waterfalls and mountains. We acknowledge deities and guardian entities that take care of the sacred sites. They have been dwelling in those places since time immemorial.

It is important to recognize the seven sacred mountain peaks, because our ancestors dwell there or they manifest there. Our rituals, celebrations, and ceremonies give thanks for what we are or ask for strength and health for ourselves, the ecosystem, and the community.

In all sacred sites, nature is combined with cultural manifestations. That is why sacred sites are biocultural. Ancestors are not physically present, but in these sacred sites we can have a more intimate and spiritual relationship with them. That is why it is important to care for and protect sacred sites—not only for today, but forever.

We should maintain the stories of creation and pass them along to our descendants, because they reflect the material and cosmogonic origin of our presence in this world. Creation stories tell us about how life first arose and how it continues to expand. They tell us about creator deities, how the Great Spirit breathed life, and how the things we see and feel were created. These stories tell us how we came to be. Creation stories are a fundamental part of understanding the mystery of life. We must preserve them and share them with future generations.

We are invited to recover our connection with the lineage through certain protocols and with the discipline required for this task. Practice reverence, respect, and responsibility with those who have given us life, beginning with the major ancestors. We were reminded of the importance of asking permission when visiting a sacred place. We were asked to remember the great task of the clans that invoke special ancestors.

Ceremonial practices help with our reconnection with the ancestors. One ceremony shared involves reconnection with the most important moments of the cycle of the day: if we stop any activity to receive the sunrise, the Sun at noon, and the sunset, we might receive the mysterious night.

We spoke here of offering ceremonies and payments in reciprocity with the beings, the entities, the deities, and everything around us, including sacred sites, mountains, volcanoes, caves, rivers, and the different beings who dwell there. We are guided to give thanks to the heart of the Earth and the heart of the sky with a short version of the ceremony of directions that helps to maintain balance and harmony with the cosmos, nature, and Mother Earth.

We learned about the practice of healing the ancestral lineage of each one of us. Investigating the history of the place where our ancestors lived and the activities they carried out is important because it reminds us of the great responsibility involved. It is vital to safeguard the wisdom that has come down to us since time immemorial so we can pass it on to future generations.

We explored some key ideas, such as the fact that we are here for a purpose, which is to take care of life and be mindful not to destroy it. Caring for life starts by honoring our ancestors. Then we will have something to offer to generations to come. We will better understand that we live with Mother Earth by only borrowing what is necessary, creating systems that give back, and never accumulating.

Life is about living in harmony and not in disharmony. We humans totally depend on Mother Earth, while Mother Earth can perhaps live without us, although our deep feeling is that she needs us in that reciprocity.

It is important to bear in mind that our identity is based on our ancestors, and that we are part of our collective identity thanks to them. We now live for them. This book realizes the importance that all humans have to acknowledge ancestors and connect with them, honoring them spiritually.

The lands and territories where we live help us remember who we truly are, why we are in this world, and where we are going. I invite you to reconnect with your ancestors and your ancestral lineages as an act of responsibility to the whole world.

Sacred sites must be preserved because they are the reflection of our ancestors. They are where life is regenerated and where our presence in the world is regenerated. They are energy points that help regenerate the life energy of all beings.

We can all clean our lineages by cleaning our actions, our thoughts, and our feelings. This process creates unification between the past and the future. Only then can we live in harmony with what life gives us.

In ceremonies, we can invite the presence of the four sacred elements of life and the four cardinal directions plus up, down, and center. This brings together the presence of heaven and Earth and the heart center of all beings.

The time is now to be at peace with the Earth and with the universe, and to recover dignity as a person, as a family, and as a community—and to remember that we are ultimately star dust. May the Great Spirit, the heart of Heaven and the heart of Earth, and the heart of beings and entities and major ancestors, bless your path.

MEET OUR SACRED STORYTELLERS

DEBORAH ANN BUSTIN continues her lifelong love affair with the power of words to process life's biggest questions, heal wounds, inspire hope, create laughter, and move people's hearts.

FLORENTINE BISSCHOPS, LLM offers keys to high-achieving pet moms who experience a sense of isolation due to feelings of not being seen for who they truly are or to express themselves in their close relationships with the confidence, joy, and strength of living in congruence with their soul. www. bubblesforyoursoul.com

LEENA BANERJEE BROWN, PH.D. is a Sukyo Mahikari member, psychologist, and author of *True Light: Ordinary People on the Extraordinary Spiritual Path of Sukyo Mahikari*. truelightbook.com

CHRIS CIEPIELA has the desire to convey the magic in the mundane through healing arts and writing. She lives in western Massachusetts with her family, Lindsay, Luca, Mateo, and their dog, Georgia.

GINNY COLARUSSO owns a yoga studio and has been practicing and teaching yoga for over fourteen years. She holds E-RYT 500 and YACEP certifications through Yoga Alliance. Ginny has mediumship abilities, is a past life regressionist, and an advanced reiki level three healer.

SUJON DATTA is an internationally renowned life architect, bioenergetic healer, and spiritual advisor. Sujon's mission is to help people open their hearts to themselves to reach their highest potential.

CHERI EVJEN is a wife, mother, and grandmother who concluded a corporate career and is now an author, certified spiritual life coach, certified grief recovery specialist, and an ordained minister with a mission to help other grandparents of child loss.

GRANDMOTHER FLORDEMAYO is a Curandera Espiritu, or a Healer of Divine Spirit. She is the founder of The Path, a 501(c)3 dedicated to the preservation of traditional knowledge and heritage seeds. Flordemayo is a founding member of the Church of the Spiritual Path, the Confederation of Indigenous Elders of the America, The International Council of Thirteen Indigenous Grandmothers, Grandmothers of the Sacred We, and The Mother Earth Delegation of United Indigenous Nations. followthegoldenpath.org and grandmotherflordemayo.com.

LUCIA GOÑEZ is a survivor healing generational trauma while integrating the strengths of her ancestors. She is passing on her strengths to her daughters as they go through their healing journeys.

J.J. HURTAK, PH.D., PH.D. AND DESIREE HURTAK, PH.D. are authors and cofounders of The Academy For Future Science, an international NGO that works to bring cooperation between science and local cultures through education with an emphasis on sustainable development. Dr. J.J. Hurtak is a social scientist and specialist in space law and cosmology and Dr. Desiree Hurtak is an environmentalist, social scientist, and futurist. futurescience. org.

DR. KURT JOHNSON is the cofounder of Light on Light Press, an imprint dedicated to interspirituality. He is one of three co-editors of *Our Moment of Choice: Evolutionary Visions and Hope for the Future,* co-author of *The Coming Interspiritual Age,* co-author of *Nabokov's Blues* and co-author of *Fine Lines.* Kurt cofounded The Interspiritual Dialogue with Br. Wayne Teasdale and is a member of the Evolutionary Leaders. lightonlight.us.

DR. JULIE KRULL serves as a midwife for the evolution of consciousness, whole-systems transformation, and a whole worldview. Working with evolutionary change-agents, she's a best-selling, Nautilus Award-winning author, speaker, creative catalyst, host of The Dr. Julie Show: All Things Connected, and founder of Good of the Whole. thedrjulieshow.com and goodofthewhole.com.

REV. YAEL NAVID is a Black Jewish feminist, fierce woman, mama, social justice midwife, community organizer, liberationist, reverend of the world, healer, mystic, public theologian, light bringer, dancer, and loud laugher. watersofoshun.org.

NINA MATHEWS is an Indian American artist yogi who works as an art therapist for the State of California. She is raising two extraordinary teenagers and a baggle named Maya.

LINDSEY ULUWEHIMAILANI MORRISS is a visionary poet and writer who believes that art and the written word can heal wounds, transform lives, and create entire cultures and realities. She knows that transformational art, writings, and expression are key ingredients for creating the better, safer, more coherent world that we all know is possible.

REV. ANNE O'NEIL is a therapist and spiritual counselor specializing in grief, trauma, and holistic wellness. She is also the author of *If You Want the Rainbow, Welcome the Rain.* yoursoulpath.com.

DR. KRISTY M. VANACORE is the author of *Rewilding: A Woman's Quest to Remember Her Roots, Rekindle Her Instincts, and Reclaim Her Sovereignty.* Known as a modern-day medicine woman, Kristy has been a prominent trailblazer in the field of holistic psychology for two decades developing an innovative approach to mind-body-spirit healing by integrating ancient wisdom with modern science. kristyvancacore.com

KAREN VAUGHAN is a road-worn adventurer who has lived in seven countries. Her stories reflect her global passion. She is currently finishing a memoir and perfecting the art of geographical independence.

SARYON MICHAEL WHITE is an author, public speaker, and channel. His first book, *Roya Sands and the Bridge Between Worlds,* is a highly relevant spiritual adventure set in the modern world. saryon.com

JUDY HELM WRIGHT is the author of over 25 books and hundreds of articles on family relationships. As a personal historian she has gathered many end-of-life stories and taught memoir classes internationally. artichokepress.com.

MEET OUR FEATURED AUTHOR

MINDAHI BASTIDA is the Director of the Original Nations Program of the Fountain, a caretaker of the philosophy and traditions of the Otomi-Toltec peoples, and an Otomi-Toltec Ritual Ceremony Officer. He is a consultant with UNESCO on issues related to sacred sites and bioculture. Mindahi has also served as Director of the Original Caretakers Program at the Center for Earth Ethics, Union Theological Seminary in the City of New York, and General Coordinator of the Otomi-Toltec Regional Council in Mexico.

Born in Tultepec, Lerma, Mexico, Mindahi holds a Doctorate of Rural Development from the Universidad Autónoma Metropolitana and an M.A. in Political Science from Carleton University, Canada. He has written and published extensively on biodiversity, Indigenous knowledge and related topics, and has taught on subjects ranging from sustainability, ethics and earth spirituality to Indigenous voices, communitarian links and intellectual property rights. Mindahi frequently lectures on Indigenous Peoples-Nation State relationships, intercultural education, sustainability and Indigenous peoples, cosmologies and philosophies of indigenous peoples, and biocultural sacred sites. He is also deeply involved with the Biocultural Sacred Sites for Humanity, Original Peoples proposal, UNESCO, the Timekeepers Program and the Process of Unification in charge of the Latin American and the Caribbean region. Mindahi is also President of the Mexico Council of Sustainable Development, a member of the Steering Committee of the Indigenous Peoples' Biocultural Climate Change Assessment Initiative, and he has served as a delegate to several commissions and summits on Indigenous rights and the environment.